WEBER ON BOWLING

DICK WEBER & ROLAND ALEXANDER

PRENTICE-HALL, Inc.   Englewood Cliffs, N.J.

Illustrations by Norm McGary and Bill Lorencz
Weber on Bowling by Dick Weber and Roland Alexander
Copyright © 1981 by Dick Weber and Roland Alexander

Printed in the United States of America

Prentice-Hall International, Inc., London
Prentice-Hall of Australia, Ptd. Ltd., Sydney
Prentice-Hall of Canada, Ltd., Toronto
Prentice-Hall of India Private Ltd., New Delhi
Prentice-Hall of Japan, Inc., Tokyo
Prentice-Hall of Southeast Asia Pte. Ltd., Singapore
Whitehall Books Limited, Wellington, New Zealand

10 9 8 7 6 5 4 3 2 1

Library of Congress Cataloging in Publication Data

Weber, Dick.
    Weber on bowling.

    1. Bowling.   I. Alexander, Roland, joint author.
II. Title.
GV903.W357   794.6   80-23649
ISBN 0-13-947937-6

To my great children,
Guy, Cindy, Ty, and Randy

—Roland Alexander

CONTENTS

ACKNOWLEDGMENTS

Bowling theory is so complicated and vast that no one man can know it all. It is for this reason that I would like to express my appreciation to the many people who actively participated in the development of this book. They gave their time and, unselfishly, their knowledge. This last point is critical. Since most of the ideas presented here cannot be found in other books, they had to be gleaned from the brighter minds who have had the patience to search out the facts for themselves in the effort to develop their games to a high professional level.

First, I want to thank Dick Weber. To have the greatest bowler in the history of professional bowling, and some say in the entire game, as a co-author is a unique privilege. I wish, here, to express my deep appreciation for his active participation in this ambitious venture of trying to capture the elusive theories of bowling in a book.

In the view of some commentators, there are bowlers who have better physical games than Dick Weber. There are some bowlers who are considered to have a better mental game than Dick Weber. But no man in the history of bowling has been able to match his ability to put both elements together and make it work over such a long period of time. His credits are outstanding.

Second, I would like to thank Dave Pearson for his knowledge and research of lane conditions. He was able to get lanesmen to talk candidly about lane maintenance techniques.

Third, I want to thank Dick Rinck for the many informative discussions we had on the subtleties of releases as they relate to lane conditions and bowling in general. Dick is one of the few experts who has worked on the various releases, and tested them on many different balls under many different conditions. His kind of specific information is very hard to obtain.

Fourth, I would like to thank my close personal friend, the outstanding West Coast professional and left-hander, Dr. Farrell Hinkle. His observations were extremely informative since they come from the side of the lane that few right-handers know or care about. His ability to analyze and then summarize complex ideas in a readable style was an invaluable contribution to this book.

Fifth, I would like to thank Al Horn, an outstanding teacher, who had a great deal to do with the formative years of Barry Asher and Bud Horn. Al was directly responsible for much of the chapter on the physical game. He also read over the rest of the manuscript and helped determine the essential material from the trivial.

Sixth, I want to thank Bud Horn. He not only proofread all the advance material in the book, but more important, he contributed his clear insights into the theoretical discussions. There are few who can bowl and analyze bowling like Bud. Additionally, his ability to add new terms and validate the professional jargon used in this book was especially appreciated. Bowling students find it acceptable to look like an amateur while trying to learn the physical part of the game, but find it embarrassing to be unfamiliar with the game's special language. We hope this book can help minimize that embarrassment.

Seventh, I would like to thank Carmen Salvino for his assistance in proofreading most of the material entitled "Professional Pointers." These short observations were designed to be not only valid but interesting. Having most of this information pass under Carmen's scrutiny was valuable for us all.

Eighth, I want to thank my dear friend Lamar Keck, a Southern California professional all-star and absolute master of the inside fall-back shot. For eight years, Lamar and I have discussed every advanced idea in this book. And more important, we have drilled over 1,000 balls for ourselves and others, demonstrating the validity of these ideas. Lamar's impeccable mind for detail expressed itself not only in drilling but in the examination of the advanced concepts in this book.

Lastly I want to thank my wife, who has given everything that a wife and partner can give throughout the development of this book. The amount of typing and retyping of the manuscript was staggering. Every valid change and addition (and there were many) to the manuscript was entered and retyped. Also, I want to thank her for her assistance in criticizing the manuscript from cover to cover. This may come as a surprise to many male-chauvinist bowlers, but my wife knows a great deal of bowling theory. When you have to sit and listen to *every* rap session on theory with touring pros over and over again, added to listening to thousands of arguments between myself and know-it-all sandbaggers, you get to KNOW bowling theory pretty well. You can appreciate the enormous patience and love that my wife is capable of when you realize that it took ten years of research (note taking and drawing diagrams) plus three years of commissioned writing (and four editors for three more years) to build this manuscript. I do indeed thank and love SUE.

Roland Alexander

INTRODUCTION

According to a Harris poll, the number of people bowling in this country increased by more than 25 percent between 1971 and 1975.

But the results of another, more recent study in 1980 weren't so encouraging. The numbers now indicated very slow growth and a lot of dropouts. The study tried to answer the question: "Why do so many bowlers quit the game after only a few years?"

After correlating its results, the study concluded that most bowlers quit because they reach a plateau. The find themselves finishing each season with the same average as the year before. They become frustrated. They can't seem to improve, so they lose interest and quit.

We feel the main reason for this disheartening experience is an information gap. The bowlers became frustrated and left the game simply because they didn't know enough about bowling to improve.

As far as they were concerned, the pin fall was a matter of chance, and lane conditions were too difficult to analyze. They further assumed that they had to bowl "their line" even if they weren't carrying strikes. Also, it rarely occurred to them that part of their problem might be the grip they were using or the way their ball was drilled.

This book attempts to show why these assumptions are false. You *can* improve your average, regardless of what you are bowling now. You can reach a level you never thought possible. All it takes is a basic knowledge of the game (which this book provides) and informed observation and practice.

Bowling is a precision game, a "just enough" game with a very small margin for error. Too much adjustment, or too little, results in failure. In sports like weight lifting, putting the shot, and sprinting, you go "all out." You expend as much effort as possible. This is not true of bowling. Bowling calls for precision, control, and "psychology."

Bowling combines some of the elements of gymnastics, basketball, and golf. Like gymnastics, bowling demands physical precision; a slight mistake in execution can result in defeat. Like basketball, bowling calls for controlled coordination of large and small muscles; a combination of vigorous effort and "touch" produces the best shot. Like golf, bowling requires mental discipline, plus a knowledge of equipment and playing surfaces.

Put these elements all together and you have a game that is beautiful to watch and fun to play. This is what makes bowling so fascinating to those who study it. We hope you will share our enthusiasm as you read and use our book. We feel it is the first complete book of basic and advanced bowling theory.

Dick Weber and Roland Alexander

1. GETTING DOWN TO FUNDAMENTALS

It is probably a good idea, right here at the beginning of our book, to lay down a few objectives. First, this is really a book of fairly advanced bowling theory. It is necessary to start with several obvious fundamentals and basic ideas in order to lay the groundwork for the more complex and advanced ideas we wish to cover.

We will spend a considerable amount of time on subjects few other bowling books tend to cover, and we will spend absolutely no time on some subjects that all other bowling books cover.

Here, you may learn for the first time, about lane conditions that may have been a mystery to you and an annoyance on those "off" nights with the league. We will discuss the "line" and how to find it; how the pins actually react and how to read them to adjust your line; and the elements of getting a proper fit with a bowling ball.

In Chapter 3, "Your Physical Game," we will discuss the elements of footwork, approach, armswing, delivery, release, and finish—and how these elements affect ball action. Finally, in chapters 9 and 10, "The Mental Game," we will discuss the psychological aspects of the game and how to think like an advanced bowler.

You will not find the usual chapters on how to keep score, or the usual diagrams on how to make spares. We feel that this information can be found in any number of other books and that there is no need to repeat it here.

Frequently, we will take the liberty of speaking to you directly when we feel the advice warrants it. We hope you don't mind our occasional preaching and an occasional sarcasm.

Okay, let's get on with it.

THE MAIN IDEA

As a bowler your goal is always to knock down the maximum number of pins with the fewest number of balls. You're allowed two chances to knock down all ten pins in each frame. Get them all with your first shot and you've got a strike. If you leave some standing after your first shot but get them all on your second, you've converted a spare.

How It's Done / Most bowlers take about four steps before putting the ball on the lane. The last step is actually a slide, during which your left foot glides forward. This is why the sole of a left bowling shoe is made of leather. (If you bowl with your left hand, the sole of your right shoe will be designed for sliding.)

The first 40 to 45 feet of the bowling lane are coated with a special oil. The rest of the lane remains dry. As a result, when the ball lands on the oiled section of the lane it begins to skid.

However, once the ball reaches the dry, non-oiled section of the lane it begins to roll. Gradually it gains traction. It takes hold and, if it has side spin, begins to revolve. The number of revolutions the ball makes varies from six to sixteen, depending on the amount of side spin given by the bowler and the traction of the ball and the lane.

Why are some parts of the lane oiled and some left dry? Well, as you might expect, it's all related to making strikes. In order to make a strike, you don't want to put the ball smack in the center of the leading pin (the headpin). You have a much better chance of knocking down all the pins if

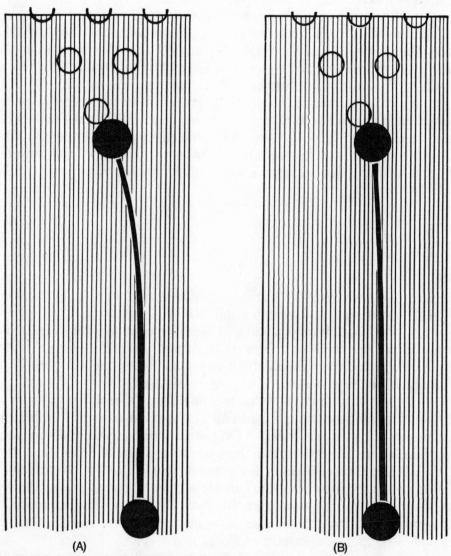

(A)　　　　　　　　　　　(B)

Figure 1–1   The size of the hook can vary. Here ball A hooked from the 10-board to the pocket (17-board), but ball B hooked only three boards—from the 14-board to the pocket

you can angle the ball between the headpin and the 3-pin with enough forward motion to start a complicated chain reaction between the ball and the pins. This requires the ball to stop skidding and begin rolling with a change of direction as it comes up to the headpin.

This prime target area of the pins is usually called the "pocket," and for the ball to end up there effectively, it must be made to hook into the pins. This is why the combination of oiled and non-oiled sections of the lane is so important. High-average bowlers don't just roll the ball down the lane. They also give it turn as they release it, producing sideroll.

But, since the ball skids for 40 or 45 feet before grabbing the dry part of the lane, the effects of this sideroll are delayed. The ball doesn't start to roll and hook (Figure 1-1) until it reaches the dry area of the lane. The arc that the ball makes as it rolls down the lane is called the "ball pattern." When a bowler throws a large arc, it is often referred to as "bellying the ball."

THE LANE

Lanes are 62 feet, 10 3/16 inches long (plus or minus 1/2 inch). They are 42 1/2 inches wide, and level to within 40/1000 inch.

Because of the pounding the lane absorbs, the front part of it is made of maple, a hardwood. So is the back part, where the falling pins give it a severe pounding. However, to give the ball more traction, the middle part of the lane is usually made of pine, a softwood.

The lane begins with the foul line. Just beyond it are a series of dots and arrows used in aiming the ball. The area between the foul line and the arrows is called the "heads." On the near side of the foul line is the "approach area." And here, too, there are several sets of dots.

The Center Board / When most people stand in the middle of the approach and look down the lane at the pins, an optical illusion distorts the alignment of the dots and the pins. Therefore, it's important to understand that the dots, arrows, and pins actually line up—they do not converge, regardless of how they appear to the eye.

As you can see (Figure 1–2), the entire lane is 39 boards wide, and the center board runs from one end of the alley to the other. The

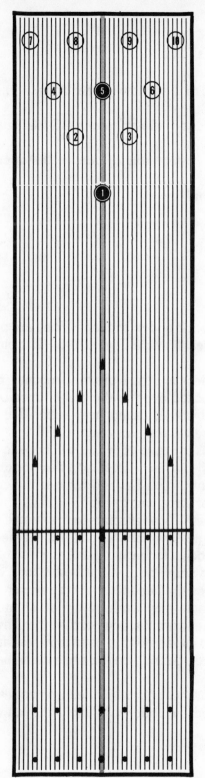

Figure 1–2   The 20-board is the center board. Like all boards, it runs the entire length of the lane. Notice the location of the dots and arrows and how they are aligned

center board is the 20-board, and all of the following markings sit squarely on it:

1. *the middle dot at the back of the approach (15 feet from the foul line)*
2. *the middle dot at the 12-foot row of dots in the approach area*
3. *the middle dot at the foul line*
4. *the 4th arrow*
5. *the headpin*
6. *the 5-pin*

THE PINS

The pins sit on the pin deck at the back end of the lane. They are placed exactly one foot apart in a symmetrical triangle (Figure 1–3). The pins are numbered one through ten.

On either side of the pin deck are the walls that become important in the chain action as pins knocked over by the ball bounce off the walls and into other pins. (This is obviously called "wall action.") Behind the pin deck is the pit that finally receives the pins and the ball.

As stated before, the idea is to make your first ball hook into the pocket between the 1-pin and the 3-pin. But just hitting the pocket isn't enough to produce strikes consistently. You have to hit it at the correct angle and with the correct amount of force and traction.

Angle at the Pocket / When a bowler refers to the "angle at the pocket," he is talking about the angle at which the ball hits the headpin (Figure 1–4). The best angle at the pocket for carrying strikes will vary from house to house and lane to lane. In some houses the best mixing action takes place when the ball approaches the headpin from the center of the lane. In other houses an outside angle may work best, that is, an angle where the ball comes up to the pocket from the edge of the lane. The only way to determine the best angle is to experiment. A change in resurfacing, oil conditions, or pin weights will have a bearing on the angle that is best for your type of shot.

Four Headpin Zones / The headpin is divided into zones. The far right side of the headpin is called the "bucket." Just to the left of the

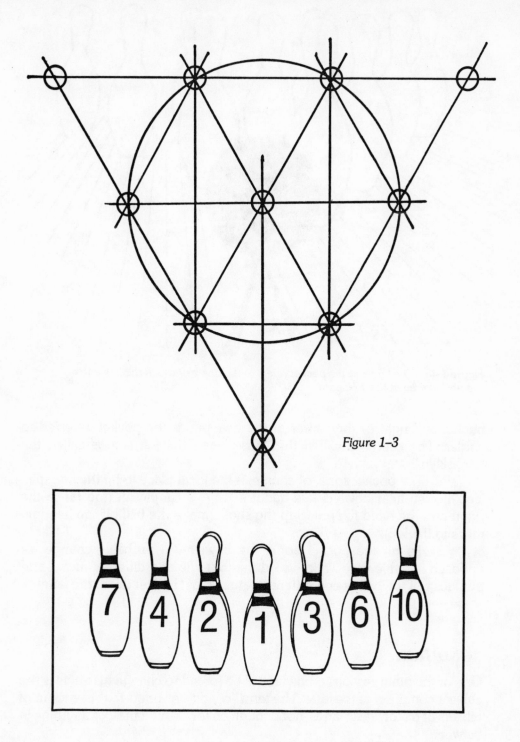

Figure 1–3

Figure 1–4   The angle at the pocket refers to the angle at which the ball enters the pocket area at the 17-board

bucket and right of the center of the headpin, is the pocket, referred to earlier. The center is called the "nose," and the left side is called the "Brooklyn."

The pocket zone, of course, is the ideal place to hit the headpin. You'll often hear bowlers talk about a "thin" headpin hit (too far to the right) and the need to "point up the shot" (make the ball hit the headpin more to the left).

To hit the pocket zone, the bowler will probably change his appoach line. He may walk toward the foul line at a different angle, and perhaps roll the ball over a different target spot (16 feet down the lane).

CONDITION

One of the main reasons a bowler will be forced to change his angle is the current condition of the lane. The term "condition" refers to the amount of oil, lots of oil for "fast" lanes, not enough oil for "slow" lanes, or anything in between.

The condition of the same lane may vary with the time of day and the amount of play. A lane is normally oiled once each day; but after it has been used, the oil will no longer be where it was originally laid down. It will have been shifted around and removed by the roll of the ball. At times the oil may be so spotty and the lane so worn that it will be very difficult to score well. This kind of condition is usually referred to as a "brickyard."

Although it is illegal, a lane can be "blocked." On a blocked lane, the oil is applied in such a way that it creates a "wall" straight to the pocket. This will be discussed in greater detail in a later chapter on lane conditions.

THREE FORMS OF POWER

There are three kinds of power that are important to every bowler: hooking power, hitting power, and carry power. Although these terms sound similar, they represent distinctly different concepts.

Hooking power is the least complicated term. It refers to the shape of the shot or the ball pattern created as the ball rolls down the lane. More specifically, it refers to how many boards your release can make the ball cross when you're throwing the ball parallel with the boards.

Hitting power refers to the ball's ability to hit the 5-pin after the headpin on pocket hits, even when heavier pins are used. The bowler creates hitting power during his release, but that power is also influenced by the lane condition in front of the pocket and on the pin deck itself.

Just as a car has greater traction on dry asphalt than on ice, so the ball has greater hitting power on a dry back end than on an oily one. This is true regardless of how strong the bowler's release is.

Carry power is the most complicated of the three terms. It refers solely to the percentage of strikes carried on headpin hits. The goal of all adjustments is to create carry power. Correct adjustments yield a high percentage of strikes when hitting the pocket with the proper amount of deflection to the right or left. Now that lighter pins with a higher center of gravity are being used, the advanced bowler's main concern is no longer the 5-pin. Now the main concern is to knock down the pocket corner pins—the 4-pin, 7-pin, and 10-pin. Thus, carry power has become more significant than hitting power. Far more potential strikes are missed by a single corner pin than by a 5-pin leave.

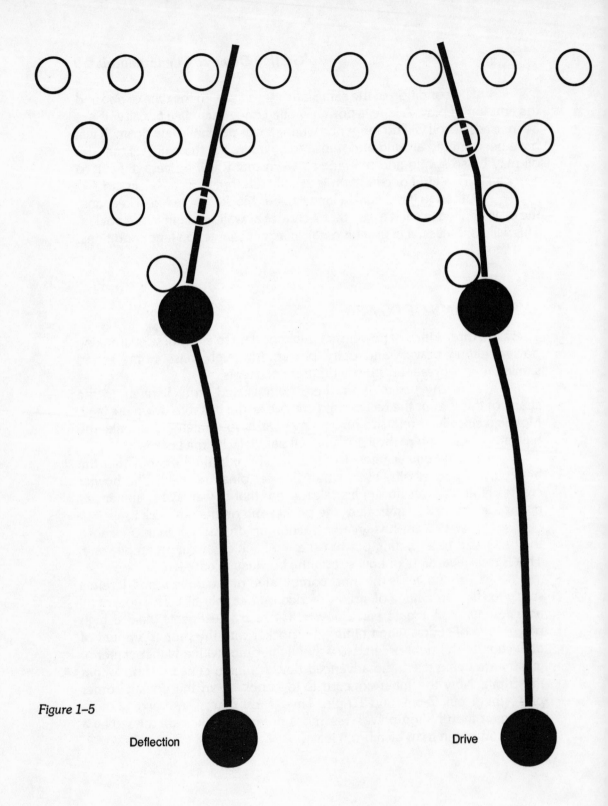

Figure 1–5

Deflection

Drive

DEFLECTION AND DRIVE

These two terms describe how the ball reacts after it hits the headpin and moves through the stack of pins. The distance the ball covers in this case is less than three feet, but it is the most crucial three feet on the entire lane.

Deflection refers to the ball's tendency to bounce off pins to the right. *Drive* refers to the ball's penetration as it drives left through the pins. (See Figure 1–5).

There are several factors that affect the deflection and drive of the ball. These include ball speed, weight of the pins, the amount and placement of oil on the lane, the composition of the ball (plastic or rubber), the angle played, and the lift or hooking power imparted to the ball while releasing it.

LIFT AND LOFT

Pure *lift* determines the number of revolutions the ball makes. The more vigorous the lift, the more revolutions. The less the lift action, the fewer revolutions. (See Figure 1–6.)

Lift is the last event in the release. Lift continues past the point of release and into the follow-through. Assume you release the ball with twist or turn. If you delay the upward direction of lifting the ball by extending your arm toward the pins, the ball will roll straighter. If you lift upward more, the ball will have more revolutions and will therefore hook more when reaching the dry area of the lane.

Loft refers to how far the ball is thrown out onto the lane beyond the foul line (Figure 1–7). If the ball hits the floor four to five feet beyond the foul line, you are using a lot of loft in your delivery. If the ball is set down near the foul line, very little loft is being used.

The more loft, the farther the ball skids. This longer skid line results in a later roll. The less the loft, the less skid the ball will have and the sooner it will roll. The drier the lane condition, the greater the need for loft. The oilier the lane, the less need for loft and the more important it is to get the ball into a roll (and out of a skid).

A bowler must learn how to regulate and control the amount of loft in his delivery. Sometimes a dozen games are bowled using the same amount of loft on each shot. Other times the amount of loft has to be

Figure 1–6   *The bowler at the top is using very little lift, so the ball tends to roll straight. The bowler at the bottom is using a lot of lift, so the ball has more revolutions and a sharper hook*

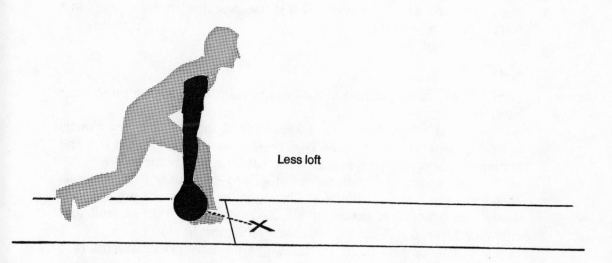

Less loft

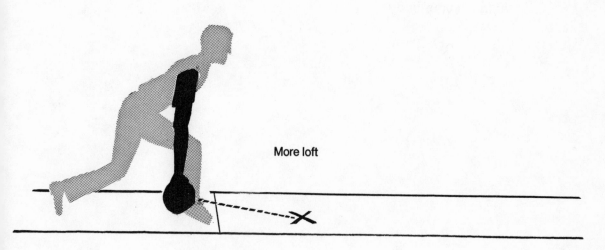

More loft

Figure 1–7

changed from shot to shot due to different lane conditions. The left lane may require a different amount of loft from the right lane in order to get lined up to score on both lanes. This is the exception, not the rule. Most pairs of lanes play evenly.

TURN

Turn refers to hand position at the time of release. There are three basic hand positions.

In the first, the hand is kept behind the ball, but not exactly behind it. This position (Figure 1–8) creates maximum forward roll and minimum sideroll, which is logical, since hardly any turn is involved.

The second hand-position (Figure 1–9) causes more sideroll. This hand position is maintained throughout the entire armswing and release, with no wrist action at all. It creates maximum sideroll and minimum forward roll (but not necessarily the most hook).

A recommendation for creating a hook with good sideroll is to stay behind the ball until the point of release (Figure 1–8). Then the wrist should be rotated counterclockwise to the hand position shown in Figure 1–9. However, be careful not to allow your elbow to fly away from the side of your body.

Figure 1–8   Keeping the hand behind the ball at the release creates maximum forward roll

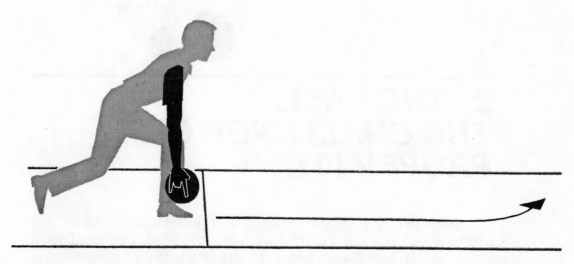

Figure 1–9   Holding the hand on the outside throughout the armswing and release will create maximum sideroll

2. THE BALL: THE CHALLENGE OF A PROPER FIT

If you want to bowl your best, the first challenge that must be met is to get a properly drilled ball. "Challenge" is an apt word, because finding someone who can drill a ball perfectly—matching both your hand and style of play—can be as difficult as making a 7–10 split.

Ball drilling is an art. And as in any field, there are people who are highly skilled, people who do a passable job, and people who are totally incompetent. No certification is required. Anyone with $1,000 dollars can buy secondhand equipment and some inventory, and call himself a ball driller. But, as the song says, "It ain't necessarily so."

Asking friends or bowling partners is one way to get the name of a good ball driller. If the driller has watched you bowl and is familiar with your game, so much the better.

16

Even though a driller comes highly recommended, you still owe it to yourself to have more than just a passing knowledge of the subject. Otherwise, you won't know what to look for or what your options are.

THE BALL—INSIDE AND OUT

All bowling balls have three parts: the outer shell, the core, and the weight block.

Shell / The outside shell (Figure 2–1) is approximately one inch thick, but this varies slightly with each manufacturer. The hardness of the shell, which also varies from one ball to another within one company, determines how much the ball grabs the lane. The softer the shell the more it grabs. It is for this reason that many bowlers use more than one ball.

Core / The core (Figure 2–2), too, varies in its composition and hardness. But the core obviously never comes into contact with the floor and the pins. Therefore, when compared to the shell and the weight block, very little consideration is given to this part of the ball by professionals.

Weight Block / The weight block (Figure 2–3) is made of a denser rubber composition. It is placed around the core prior to putting on the outer cover. If you shine a flashlight into the thumb or finger holes, you might see the weight block. Certain manufacturers use a different color for the weight block in plastic colored balls. Of the three elements that make up a bowling ball, the weight block used to be the most important factor to consider when drilling. However, starting in the late 1970s, manufacturers began making soft-shelled balls. Previously, almost all rubber balls were approximately the same hardness, as measured with a hardness meter. The range appeared to be from low 80's to high 80's. Current manufacturers produce balls with shell hardness measuring from the low 70's to low 90's. A ball registering 72 is softer than one registering 90. The 72 will outhook the 90 by a wide margin.

Because of this it appears that now the shell has more influence than the weight block over the amount of hook. The placement of the weight block in relation to the grip influences the ball pattern (how far the ball skids and hooks).

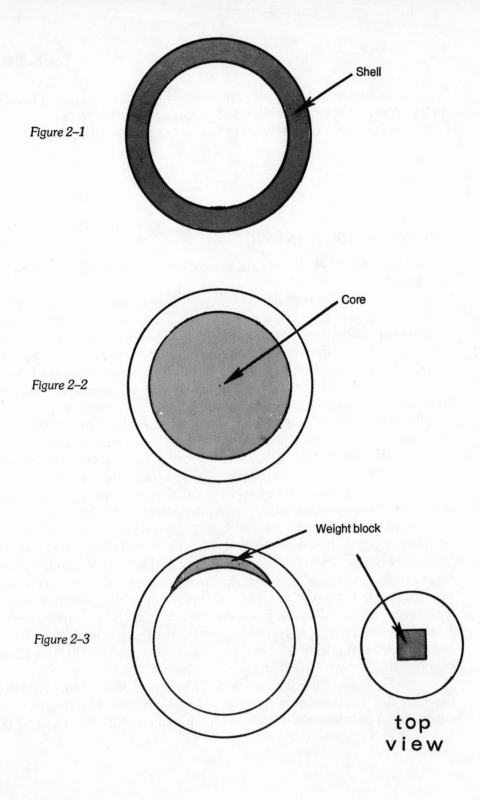

Figure 2–1

Shell

Figure 2–2

Core

Figure 2–3

Weight block

top
view

FIVE DRILLING FACTORS

There are five factors to be considered when drilling a ball:
1. *the hardness of the shell (just discussed above)*
2. *the width of the holes (size)*
3. *the arrangement of the holes (span)*
4. *the angle of the holes (pitch)*
5. *the depth of each hole (grip)*

All five measurements are related. If one is changed, it has an effect on what the other measurements should be. For example, deep holes require a smaller span. Since a larger part of each finger is inside the ball, the distance between the thumb and finger holes cannot be the same as that used for shallow holes. This is true when one contrasts a conventional and a full fingertip grip.

Size / The size of each hole should be comfortable and snug enough for controlling the ball, but not so tight that the fingers won't come out easily.

Generally, the size of the thumb hole should be approximately 3/64 inch greater than the smallest hole you can cram your thumb into without getting it stuck. (Note: drills come in 1/64 differences, e.g., 3/4, 49/64, 25/32, 51/64, etc.)

If, for example, a hole measuring 15/16 inch is the smallest you can cram your thumb into, then three sizes up from that is 63/64. This is not necessarily the thumb hole you should use, but it is a good reference point to start with.

The driller should have drills measuring 1/64 differences. If he doesn't, and has only drills in the 1/32s, and your finger sizes fall in between, then he will either drill the holes too large or too small.

If he drills them too big, you will have to put pieces of electrician's tape inside the back of the holes to tighten them up. If the holes are drilled too small, then each hole will have to be worked out with a three-cornered knife very skillfully. If instead, the driller chooses to sand out the necessary difference with an electric sander, then the holes will feel "mushy." This is caused by removing too much material near the surface of the ball and not enough farther down. This procedure is not recommended, since it will reduce the amount of feel in your fingertips when you release the ball. And *feel* is what you try to obtain by practicing!

Span / The "span" (Figure 2–4) is the distance between the thumb and finger holes. With your thumb all the way inside the thumb hole, place the rest of your hand on top of the ball with the fingers lying across the holes. The crease on each finger should lie across the middle of each hole. The span must be drilled correctly, for if it's wrong, your hand will tire before two games are bowled. Also, this sort of error will prevent developing the "feel" needed to bowl consistently high scores.

Bridge / The distance between the finger holes is called the "bridge" (Figure 2–5). Usually this distance measures 1/4 inch or 3/8 inch, although some advanced bowlers use very narrow bridges of 1/8 inch or 1/16 inch.

Generally speaking, bowlers who like to hook the ball prefer a wider bridge, while those who like a straight shot prefer a narrower bridge.

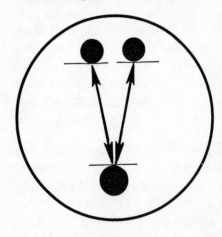

Figure 2–4   Since there are two finger holes, there are actually two spans. Usually, though, the term refers to the average distance between the two finger holes and the thumb hole.

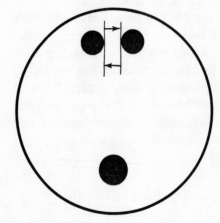

Figure 2–5   Bridge

Pitches / You would assume that all bowlers would want pitches drilled for comfort, if nothing else. But a few bowlers believe in experimenting with pitches that let their hand out of the ball only when they have made a perfect release. This is called the "punishing grip," because when the slightest error is made in the release, the ball hangs up on your thumb, causing excruciating pain. If you want to practice with a ball drilled like this, that's your business. But for obvious reasons, it doesn't work well in competition (the screaming distracts other bowlers).

The pitch *should* be drilled for comfort. It should allow control of the ball throughout the entire arm swing and release. You should not have to fight to hold on to it. But at the same time, the ball shouldn't hang up while you're releasing it.

The amount of pitch selected will naturally depend on the flexibility of your fingers and your style of play. But to give some idea of what the choices are, here are some of the most common pitches and how they can influence the shot.

Under Pitch / This kind of pitch (Figure 2–6) allows a more closed hand grip. Its advantage is that it will enhance the ball spin by permitting more lift. Bowlers who throw big hooks favor underpitch in the fingers. But too much underpitch can cause your hand to drag coming out of the ball. Also, it can unintentionally cause increased loft and reduce your accuracy.

Reverse Pitch / This pitch (Figure 2–7) permits an open grip. It encourages an earlier release and more forward roll, and it reduces finger lift. A straight-line ball shooter is more likely to favor reverse pitches. But too much reverse pitch can force the bowler to squeeze the ball out of fear of dropping it.

Reverse Thumb Pitch / This is the most common thumb (Figure 2–8) pitch among top players and it makes it easier to get the thumb out of the ball earlier than the fingers. This is extremely important when throwing a ¾ roller.

Under Thumb Pitch / This pitch (Figure 2–9) yields a better grip on the ball, but it can make it difficult to let go in time. It is not commonly used among high-average bowlers. Most older house-balls were drilled with under pitches.

For years it was assumed that bowlers with large hands also had strong hands—and therefore that they were the only ones who could use reverse pitch in the thumb and fingers—while bowlers with small hands

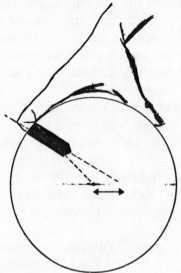

Figure 2–6   Under pitch

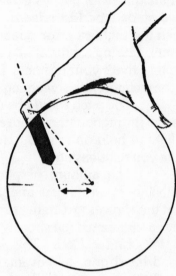

Figure 2–7   Reverse pitch

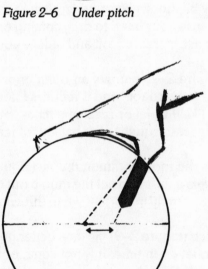

Figure 2–8   Reverse-thumb pitch

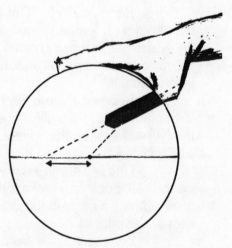

Figure 2–9   Under-thumb pitch

required underpitch to help them hold onto the ball. Some drillers still follow this belief. But after analyzing the grips of touring professionals, it shows bowlers with small hands using pitches similar to those used by bowlers with large hands. It's just a matter of what works best for each bowler.

Lateral Pitches / It is also possible to drill a ball with left or right lateral pitch. In these cases, the holes are angled slightly to the left or right, instead of straight downward. Lateral pitches are used primarily to compensate for crooked fingers. (Many people's fingers toe-in slightly at the first joint—look at your own fingers.)

It is impossible to make any rules about these pitches, since they are related to personal comfort. In a few cases, lateral pitch is used to enhance a special release the individual bowler believes he can make with it.

Grip / The depth of the hole is determined by the kind of grip you use. There are two standard grips: the conventional and the full fingertip ("tip"). All other grips are customized variations that are designed to alter the ball pattern, or to make allowances for some unique characteristic of the hand.

You may hear these specialized configurations called the semi-tip, the flesh-tip, the Collier, the Williams, the Bates grip, and so forth. If you are interested in them, ask your pro. However, I find that for most people the conventional or the full-tip work best.

The Conventional Grip / This grip (Figure 2–10) permits the bowler to put his fingers into the ball up to the second knuckle. If a good hold on the ball is required, use a conventional grip.

There are some advantages and disadvantages that you should know about. Except for bowlers like Wayne Zahn and Glenn Allison, this grip usually produces a straighter ball than the full tip. That makes it great for picking up spares, but it makes it harder to create hooking and hitting power. On an oily lane or one with heavy pins, it may be difficult to hit the pocket with the force needed to produce a good mixing action among the pins.

The Full Fingertip / This grip (Figure 2–11) allows the fingers to be put into the ball only up to the first joint, and it requires a strong hand. Like the conventional, it has both advantages and disadvantages.

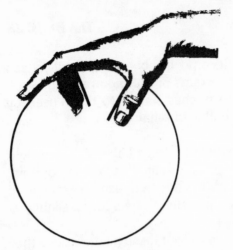 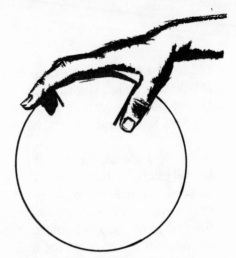

Figure 2–10   Conventional grip   *Figure 2–11   Full-fingertip grip*

On the plus side are the increased hitting power and the greater variety of ball patterns. On the minus side, this ball is harder to control. The full tip will skid less and hook more. It reacts more quickly to the varying lane conditions, which makes mastering this ball more complex.

But the full fingertip can produce greater hitting power, which is fine under most conditions. However, there are times when increased hitting power becomes a disadvantage. For instance, on very dry lane conditions and very light pins you may find that the ball has too much hitting power but not enough carrying power.

The pins should hit each other where they are the widest—in the bellies. When too strong a ball overpowers light pins, this belly-to-belly action is reduced. The pins fly up into the air, causing key pins to pass by the narrow neck of the next pin rather than hitting the wide belly. The most notable key pin pass is when the 6–pin misses the 10–pin on a pocket hit.

Yet, contrary to popular opinion, it isn't necessary to have a high average before trying a full fingertip. In fact, you may be holding your average down by not learning how to throw it.

So I'd suggest drilling a used ball with a full-fingertip grip. Then practice with it until you're comfortable. Once that point has been reached, consider buying a new ball and having it drilled for the full-fingertip grip.

But in the meantime, don't throw away your old conventional ball, and don't have it plugged! There will be times when the lanes are so dry that you'll need it. Don't burn your bridges.

BALL WEIGHT DISTRIBUTION

Every ball has a weightblock, usually located directly under the label. Its primary purpose is to compensate for the weight of the material removed by drilling. But by knowing where to drill the grip in relation to the weight block, the ball can be given a slight weight bias that will affect the ball pattern and hitting power. While this is not as significant to ball patterns as the release and the shell hardness, it does make some difference and can be used as an advantage. *But* a bowler who doesn't hook the ball big won't be able to hook a ball "out of the building" or throw as much hook as, say, Mark Roth, no matter how the ball is weighted. *Release dominates weights*.

Weight biases are referred to as positive, negative, finger, thumb, top, and bottom weight. Thus, a drilled ball can be thought of as having six "sides." A zero-weighted ball is drilled so that there is no weight bias at all. The following examination of each bias, however, does not refer to carry power. Carry power is a function of your entire lineup, of which hitting and hooking power are but two elements. Carry power is the bottom line to the question: Am I getting a lot of strikes?

Positive Weight / Helps (Figure 2-12) the ball to skid through the heads, increases hitting power at the pocket, and makes the ball hook more at the back end (near the pins). It is called "positive" weight because when the ball is released the weight block is off center to the side nearer the headpin.

Generally speaking, positive weight increases the ball's tendency to skid before "grabbing" the lane (skid line). It also increases hooking and hitting power.

Negative Weight / Helps (Figure 2–13) the ball get into a roll sooner (shortens the skid line), decreases hitting power at the pocket, and makes the ball hook less on the back end. This happens because the weight block is on the side away from the 5-pin (the right) as the ball rolls up to the pocket.

The driller must be careful, however, when lateral pitches are involved. If the driller maps out the ball to create positive weight and then drills a right lateral pitch, he may remove enough core material from the right of center to cancel out the positive weight he was trying to achieve.

Finger vs. Thumb Weight / Figure 2–14 shows that the thumb half of the ball is heavier than the finger half. To get this weight, the thumb hole is drilled closer to the center of the weight block than the finger holes.

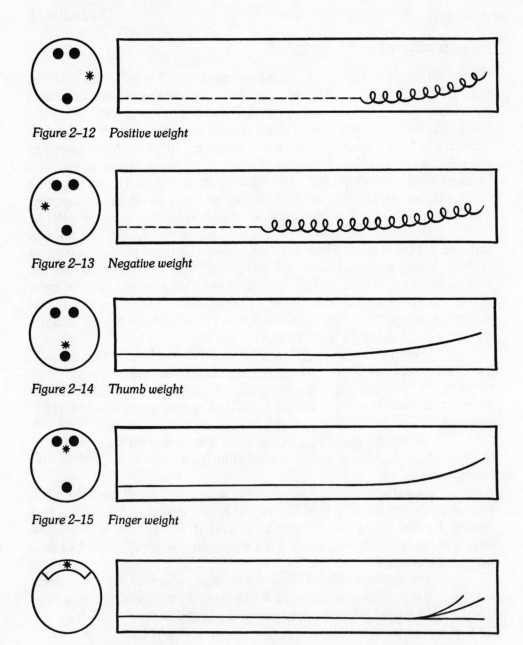

Figure 2–12   Positive weight

Figure 2–13   Negative weight

Figure 2–14   Thumb weight

Figure 2–15   Finger weight

Figure 2–16   Top weight

ABC rules state that the weight difference can be no greater than one ounce. The most dramatic weight change in ball pattern is created by altering your finger or thumb weights. Thumb weight will produce a smoother, more softly arcing hook, while finger weight (Figure 2–15) will make the ball hook more sharply.

In order to drill a ball with finger or thumb weight, the driller must calculate (with the aid of charts) how much material will be removed in the finger and thumb holes. It is not easy for a driller to give the exact amount of finger or thumb weight requested, due to complicated estimates of the amount of weight removed in drilling each hole. But you should expect it to be accurate within ⅛ ounce. (He should be able to get exact side weights by using a "dodo scale.")

Top vs. Bottom Weight / Figure 2–16 shows the ball to have top weight, even after drilling. In an undrilled ball, the weight block creates top weight ranging from 2 to 5 ounces. Once the ball has been drilled, there cannot be a difference of greater than 3 ounces from top side to bottom side. For example, before drilling, a 16-pound ball may weigh anywhere from 15 pounds 9 ounces to 16 pounds 2 ounces.

Assume for a moment that the label on the box describing ball weight is correct (this isn't always true, so it is wise to have the ball weighed before purchasing it). Further, assume the label says the ball weighs 16 pounds exactly, with 4 ounces top weight. This means that the bottom half of the ball weighs 7 pounds 14 ounces, while the top half weighs 8 pounds 2 ounces.

The extra weight provided by the weight block will compensate for the loss of weight when the ball is drilled. If there were no weight block, there would always be extra bottom weight of 2 to 3 ounces, which is undesirable. In fact, very few bowlers have success with bottom weight.

Top weight exaggerates the ball's reaction to speed and release. A ball that has 2 to 3 ounces of top weight will react more to changes in speed than a ball that has zero top weight. The amount of top weight is determined by how much of the weight block was removed in drilling.

3. YOUR PHYSICAL GAME: FOOTWORK AND ARMSWING

FOOTWORK

If you are a beginning bowler, it is highly recommended that you start out with the four-step approach. This is the "classic" way of delivering the ball, and all other footwork patterns are derived from it.

A three-step approach, for example, is actually a compressed version of the four-step. The main difference is that you have to swing the ball faster because you cover fewer steps before the release. And there will be less time to correct any errors made at the beginning of the pushaway.

A five-step approach is merely the four-step with an extra step tacked on. Thus, in a five-step approach the ball is carried for a stride before beginning the armswing. Five-step bowlers claim they have more time in the delivery position while making the shot. But some also claim they have more timing problems.

As you become experienced, one of these two approaches may work better. But because the four-step is the most unified of all approaches, and since it works so well for so many bowlers, you should try it first.

It is possible to develop an unorthodox style and become a PBA Champion. However, for every bowler who successfully puts together all the necessary physical compensations for an unorthodox championship style, there are hundreds of thousands of bowlers who wish they had learned a simpler, more straightforward style.

THE FOUR STEPS

Here then is a brief description of the four-step approach, followed by a more detailed analysis of the four distinct positions involved.

Stance / Stand about four and a half steps behind the foul line. The half step is for the slide. Your feet should be placed side by side in a normal standing position—or with the left foot slightly ahead of the right, pointing in the direction of your "target" spot. Knees slightly bent, your weight should be supported on the left foot just before stepping off, so it will be easier to shift the weight to the right foot on the first step. The ball should be held with both hands supporting its weight. Hold the ball with the forearm level with the floor, pointing at the target. The ball should be held close to the side of your body. With the ball in this position it is possible to push the ball forward toward the target, allowing the ball to swing backward and forward in a smooth pendulum motion.

Your starting position may change as you gain experience and learn to adjust to lane conditions.

Eventually, where you stand will depend upon: (1) normal approach distance, (2) conditions requiring a change from normal ball speed, and (3) the angle being played at the time.

For example, when the lanes are oily, some bowlers use a shorter approach than on dry lanes. This maneuver slows their ball speed, which allows the ball to roll earlier. (Ever throw a ball that skids the entire length of the alley? What a helpless feeling that is!)

Having the weight already resting on the left foot makes it possible to take the first step with the right foot, without shifting your weight. This eliminates the possibility of throwing your arm out of line with the target. But do what is comfortable. The first step can be a short one, ten to fifteen inches. The second and third steps should be of normal walking-stride length. The fourth step (with the left foot) is a sliding step (knee bent as deeply as is comfortable), somewhat longer than steps two and three, with the body leaning forward. The right leg automatically becomes a balance beam helping to hold the body stationary throughout the trigger position and follow-through. If you are forced to decelerate your footwork in order to be in time with your armswing, then you've rushed the line—a flaw.

First Step / When you are positive about what you want to do, begin your approach.

The first step is very important because it sets the pace and direction of the approach. A slow and deliberate first step in the desired direction helps avoid rushing the line or drifting. When the first step is too fast or in the wrong direction, compensations will have to be made later in the approach.

The most common mistake made by professional and amateur bowlers is rushing the line. This error usually results from not positioning yourself properly before starting the approach, and then beginning with too rapid a first step.

Second Step / The second step may be slightly longer and faster than the first. However, don't exaggerate these differences, because they will occur without conscious effort. Continue to walk, heels down first, straight toward your target, and at a slow pace.

Third Step / The third step is marked by increasing length and (in some styles) speed, but you must concentrate on walking straight. Compensations in timing are frequently made in this step. A short, rapid step or hop is common. These compensations attempt to achieve proper timing to enter the fourth step and point of release.

Fourth Step / Entering the fourth step, the upper body must be leaning forward. The bowler pushes off with his right foot to go into a slide on his left foot. The push-off is the last accelerating step of the approach, and it greatly influences the body momentum the bowler will carry into his point-of-release position.

As the weight shifts from the right foot to the left foot the hips should be "unblocked" by shifting or clearing them to the left. Barry Asher, a top-flight touring professional, demonstrates this well. The clearing of the hips will allow the armswing to continue in a vertical line without interference with your left leg.

During the push-off the left knee will bend. This flexibility of the knee will allow the leg to absorb the change in body momentum from its greatest speed to a standstill. It will give the bowler varying degrees of leverage, depending upon his timing when entering the leverage position. Most low-average bowlers fail to bend their left knees enough. Consequently, they can't get enough leverage to throw a good ball (Wayne Webb notwithstanding).

There are three basic footwork patterns within the four-step approach. The first method is to take four evenly spaced steps throughout. Bowlers like Bud Horn do not change the distance between steps in their approach to the line.

In the second method, there is a variation in the third step (right foot), where some bowlers use a short, quick, timing step before their slide to help correct advanced timing.

In the third method, the bowler uses a pattern in which the four steps increase in length sequentially, i.e., second step longer than the first, third step longer than the second. This will occur unconsciously for most bowlers, due to increased momentum developed in the approach. Setting your heels down first as you walk will avoid accelerating the approach.

Usually the first step is under twenty inches in length. However, stars such as Don McCune and Roy Buckley have been successful with longer initial steps.

ARMSWING

The starting position of the ball helps determine the path of armswing, ball speed, and the amount of hook.

If the ball is held too close to the middle of the body, the arm will tend to swing away from the body in the backswing. This is the result of the natural pendulum action of the arm. Assume the shoulder is stable and the arm is a string with a weight attached to its end. If the weight is pulled forward (ideally in the direction of the target) and allowed to swing freely, it will continue to swing back and forth on that line because that was the direction originally given to it.

But if the weight had been swung forward but slightly to the left of the target, then the weight would swing to the right in the backswing and to the left in the downswing. Some bowlers have learned to compensate for this kind of pushaway by looping the ball in their backswing. If this delivery is grooved and they win titles, it must be right for them. But it is a compensation that requires hundreds of hours to incorporate successfully.

The principle of looping is also applicable when the ball is held too far to the right. The armswing will tend to move behind the body on the backswing.

Bowlers who start from either of these positions must compensate in their armswings to allow the ball to be brought forward along the intended line. Thus, they must loop in the backswing the same as a golfer does, and for the same reason. The golfer must get the club head moving along the intended line of flight when the ball is hit.

Therm Gibson was a great advocate of starting the ball to the right of his body. This allowed his armswing to clear his hips without introducing any compensatory looping. Therm was a big man with large hips, and this technique worked well for him, although other bowlers who adopted this style found it detrimental to their consistency. Dave Soutar, one of the most accomplished bowling professionals, had bowled well for years while starting the ball to the right of his body.

Another error may be eliminated by keeping the right elbow snug against the body when taking your stance. (Don Carter used this technique successfully.) If the elbow is allowed to swing away from the body it will introduce a lateral motion into the armswing. Carmen Salvino has been noted for his flying elbow; however, he stands alone as one who has been able to incorporate this armswing movement. Carmen is exceptionally talented and is able to make an unorthodox move come out right. It's not likely that he would recommend it for the rest of us.

PUTTING IT ALL TOGETHER

Take a relaxed but firm stance. Fix your eyes on the target spot—not the pocket, but the arrows—approximately 16 feet down the lane. Start the ball on the pushaway ever so smoothly and bring your right foot forward at the same time. Try not to rush your footwork, and avoid hopping on the third step. Try bending at the waist in steps two and three. Remember: the more you bend, the less stress occurs to your shoulder at the height of your backswing. Otherwise there will be a tendency to swing your arm away to the right.

Allow the ball to continue its natural pendulum swing when walking to the line. As you start the fourth step the ball begins its downswing. As the foot slides to a stop, the ball will reach its lowest point.

The ball will now be just slightly behind the foul line. This is the time to exert a bit of power, but always in a direct line to the target. Remember, power should be applied smoothly, not with a yank or a jerk. Never try to increase the normal speed of the ball suddenly, since this will cause the ball to veer from its natural swing.

Never set up timing so that you have to decelerate your armswing. Trying to hold back on a shot is difficult, and is also defensive bowling. In fact, it is better to accelerate your armswing slightly throughout the point of release. This provides more control. It is the same principle used in golf when chipping or lag putting (short putts can be stroked evenly). Always accelerate through the stroke for control, never decelerate.

When the ball leaves your hand, your arm should continue to swing toward the target, then upward in an arc. Now the elbow can bend.

Continue to hold your position, or "post the shot," until the ball rolls over the target spot about 15 feet beyond the foul line. Only then may you take your eyes off the target to watch the ball on its way to the pocket.

THE FOUR POSITIONS

There are four positions to every bowler's style. At one time or another at least one of these positions has caused problems, even for great bowlers. In order to build a solid physical game, every bowler has had to take his game apart, experiment with one or another of these positions, and rebuild his style to include a "new" move. What you see at professional tournaments are movements that are fluid, continuous, and unified. What you haven't seen are the endless hours of painstaking practice sessions. The more effortless a style appears, the more likely it is that the bowler has worked long hours on his game.

Nelson Burton, Jr., is considered to be one of the world's smoothest bowlers, and he also has the reputation of being one of the hardest practicers in the game. Since even professionals spend so much time practicing on specific positions, it's important to spend a little more time on the elements and variations of each. The four positions are:

1. *Pushaway*
2. *Backswing*
3. *Trigger Position*
4. *Post Position*

Pushaway / The pushaway (Figure 3–1) is the first part of the moving physical game. It starts the timing between the armswing and footwork. A bad start leads to a bad finish, unless some compensating movements are introduced somewhere along the way to "bail out" the shot. When this is done, however, consistency is immediately forfeited. Therefore, always start the ball slowly, and start your footwork slowly.

There are two pushaway problems involved that never seem to leave a bowler's game, permanently, and they usually recur under pressure.

The first is rushing the foul line—a direct result of rushing the pushaway. Remember, the pushaway is not only arm movement; it includes the first step as well.

This "first moving part" can have other difficulties, but they are easier to control. You might start your pushaway off line, usually to the right of your shoulder. Or, you may pump the pushaway (get too energetic), but usually these problems can be corrected with practice.

The second problem is carrying the ball, not getting it started at the same time as the first step. When expert bowlers tighten up, and are aiming shots by being too careful, there is a tendency to overemphasize each physical movement. Since the pushaway is the first moving part, they tend to hold the ball too long, even after the start of their footwork.

Barry Asher was fighting this very problem during a 1975 winter tour. He had been trying to control it for months. It got so bad that it appeared he not only couldn't start properly but couldn't start at all. On a major network televised tournament he fidgeted, he hesitated, he shuffled. He would start, then stop. (It should be added, though, that even his pushaway problem didn't keep him from winning the tournament.)

If the approach is begun with the ball near your knees, more muscle and more bending forward of the body are usually required to achieve a backswing that is high enough. Carmen Salvino and Wayne Webb demonstrated this best (in 1980) by holding the ball at their sides with their right arms straight. Neither required compensative movements.

If the body is generally erect in the beginning, with the ball held waist high or higher, very little muscle exertion will be needed in the backswing because of the ball momentum developed from the higher starting position. However, the more vigorous the pushaway, the more difficult it is to control the whole approach, because the ball swings you. This is especially prominent with women bowlers who use a ball that is too heavy.

Figure 3–1   The pushaway

Backswing / The backswing (Figure 3–2) is the second moving part of the physical game, and it is equally important. You hear many people at a tournament saying, "He's scoring OK, but he's still got a bad armswing."

The backswing can have a number of variations and still be functionally correct for a given style. The purists claim that any armswing to the left or right of straight back is a flaw, but this is an oversimplification.

In analyzing any mechanical movement, you must ask: How consistent is it? How adjustable is it? And how dependable is it? Could anyone claim Earl Anthony has a bad armswing just because he bends his elbow in the backswing?

Consistency produces strings of strikes. An adjustable armswing increases your range. Dependability insulates against pressure. If your armswing has these attributes, you're on your way to becoming a first-rate bowler.

Only a few of the most classic armswings in the world have won as often as one that was less than classic. Remember Don Carter's armswing? Obviously, there is more to scoring than just this one part of the physical game.

Once a bowler has established a winning physical game, his backswing isn't necessarily free of problems forever. On the contrary, he may go weeks without trouble, and then, because of a change of condition in a different house, he begins altering his backswing to alter his speed.

The higher the backswing the greater the ball speed; the lower the backswing the slower the ball. Rarely, however, will an expert bowler alter the backswing to circle more behind his back, or take the backswing further away from his body. Doing something like this can be disastrous to the bowler's critical armswing pattern. Even if it worked for one kind of condition, it wouldn't be worth the disorientation it would cause in the bowler's game. It would sacrifice long-term benefits for immediate gains.

This leads to the final fact about the backswing: Whatever your natural swingline is—slightly outside, slightly inside, straight back, or a small loop—once that pattern is grooved, any departure from your natural swingline constitutes an error for your game. Adjustments in the backswing should be confined to those affecting speed, not direction. That is, the backswing may be adjusted higher or lower, faster or slower. But it is extremely hazardous to adjust your backswing from side to side.

Figure 3–2   The backswing

Trigger Position / The trigger position (Figure 3-3) is the third part of the physical game. The trigger point in bowling is analogous to the point where a golf club meets the ball, or where a baseball meets the bat. It is the "point of no return," the critical moment at which the destiny of the ball is determined. All preliminary movements have set the stage for this moment.

If you look very closely you'll discover that despite the wide difference in approach styles among expert bowlers, they look similar in the trigger position. Their stances may vary radically; their backswings may be different; their follow-throughs may be unusual; but they all end up in a similar trigger position. It's the same in baseball and golf: there are many different prior movements, but at the point of impact, notice how similar they all look.

The trigger position is potentially the most problem prone of all four parts of the physical game. All preliminary errors for which there was no successful compensation show up in the trigger position. Timing problems, upper-body position problems, armswing problems, and release problems all have their effect here. Timing may be off because you're ahead or behind your armswing. You may not achieve a deep enough knee bend and provide good leverage on the shot; therefore, your ball will lack hitting power. Sliding properly may be difficult because you have reached the line with your body too erect or leaning backwards, causing the rubber heel on your left shoe to grab or stick. (Often bowlers complain about sticky approaches, but they caused the sticking.)

Moreover, bad timing can force the ball to be lost on the downswing and deprive your shot of lift and turn. Or bad timing can force you to top the ball (this means your thumb has rotated left during the release all the way to the six o'clock position), causing you to think you have a release problem.

Upper-body problems are just as devastating. You may reach the trigger position too erect, so that extension on the shot is lost. This not only knocks out your control but changes your ball pattern, causing it to hook too early. You might block the shot by failing to unblock your hips. Then you may be bending at the waist, instead of at the knee. This results in the false impression that you are getting terrific leverage on the shot. It appears this way because your head, and thus your eyes, are closer to the floor.

Figure 3–3   The trigger action

Armswing problems climax in the trigger position. If the armswing was too far inside (behind you), then this results in trying to correct your armswing by "roundhousing"—flaring your arm away from your side (you also miss your target to the right). If your backswing was too far outside (away from your body) then you will try to fight pulling the ball to the left by veering your stroke out to the right. You can avoid all of this by creating a loop in your backswing, but this is definitely not advisable. Substituting one compensation for another does not equal doing it correctly.

Jim Stefanich, another outstanding tour player, had been fighting an armswing problem longer than Barry Asher had been fighting his push-away problem. Credit their talent that they both can shoot a "300" game and win PBA tournaments while contending with these obstacles. Stefanich found that if he could keep a sponge (beneath his shirt) high under his arm throughout the shot, then this proved that he hadn't allowed his armswing to leave his side. He did this trick during the 1975 season and was observed on TV still doing it in 1976.

This isn't meant to criticize two great bowlers; their problems are mentioned only to point out that even the top experts have to contend with execution difficulties even while winning. Like professionals and leading amateurs, every bowler must continue to look for solutions to his problems if he intends to improve his game.

Post Position / The post position (Figure 3–4) is the final part of your physical game. The term comes from the idea of a post in the ground—"hitting the line as solid as a post." This position is less "cause" and more "effect." Since the ball has already left your hand, whatever is done now is an aftereffect. But this does not mean that what occurs after clearing the shot is unimportant. How you finish indicates how you executed the earlier positions. If you were off balance in the trigger position, then you will be off balance in the follow-through. If you cut the shot off early in the trigger position, your follow-through will be diminished. If you rushed the line in your footwork, you'll end up with an ice skater's finish (an ice skater slides sideways when coming to an abrupt stop).

There are three techniques for finishing the shot after the point of release. The first is the classic post position as used by Bud Horn, Nelson Burton, Jr., and Dave Davis. As the right foot pushes off, the left knee

Figure 3–4   The post position

bends, and the hips are slid to the left. This allows a free and straight right armswing and follow-through, with the body position changing very little following the ball release. The right leg now acts as a balance beam, helping the body remain stationary throughout the trigger position.

The second method of finishing the shot is the right-side follow-through, demonstrated by Carmen Salvino and myself. As the ball is delivered, the right side and leg come forward alongside until the feet and shoulders are perpendicular to the ball path. This is a natural consequence of a free-wheeling style. But often amateurs fail to execute the proper knee bend before completing the shot in this style. They don't bend the left leg sufficiently. When the knee is deeply bent in posting the shot, the leg can absorb the change in momentum from maximum speed to a standstill. But if the leg is stiffened, its potential for absorbing momentum is minimized and the body spins sideways toward the foul line, with few exceptions.

The third technique for finishing the shot past the point of release is demonstrated by Larry Laub. It is a straightening-up style. As the bowler finishes the slide, his body motion changes direction from forward to upward, thus absorbing body momentum. Larry combines this movement with a high follow-through to complete his approach.

One comment might be made here in defense of all those great bowlers whose styles contain what others consider to be flaws." When a bowler builds a tournament-winning style that is grooved and permits him to make all the necessary adjustments to win, then it is absurd to criticize his game. But you shouldn't adopt the idiosyncrasies of his style if they are unnatural for you.

TIMING

Timing is the combination of footwork, body position, and armswing. How these factors relate to each other at given points in the approach will vary tremendously from bowler to bowler. Differences in timing are most apparent at the point of release. In general, a hooker (a bowler who likes to hook the ball a lot) will have his sliding foot halt prior to ball delivery, while a stroker will release the ball while his foot is still sliding.

Barry Asher and Jim Godman are hookers who post their shots, whereas Mark Roth explodes from this position. However, each type will stop his sliding foot to establish a firm base against which he can pull or accelerate the ball through the final stages of the downswing. This solid base provided by the left foot is like the firm left side suggested for golfers, which permits increased leverage on the shot.

Bowlers such as Dick Ritger and Earl Anthony bowl well by stroking on the slide. This type of bowler establishes less position to pull against, reducing the amount of the additional torque and driving power exhibited by the hooker. The strokers usually throw a softer shot with increased accuracy. Hookers will use more of the pocket in carrying strikes, whereas strokers pack the pocket more often (blowing the rack straight back without using the wall).

One must appreciate the individuality of timing. The normal relationship between body position, armswing, and footwork will depend on the style of the bowler. Although many bowling instructors recommend that beginners try to develop a timing pattern that brings the ball and sliding foot to the foul line simultaneously, this relationship would not work for Mark Roth. In fact, it would imply that either Mark's armswing was abnormally fast or his footwork unusually slow. But if Roth's timing were exhibited by Dick Ritger, the reverse problem would be present. That is, Ritger's feet would be ahead of his armswing, for his style.

Bowlers have different natural timing relationships, therefore, each person must learn what is normal and successful for him or her.

Before leaving the physical execution section, a cautionary comment is warranted. Everyone believes that he can teach someone else to bowl. Moreover, it doesn't seem to matter to the "teacher" if he himself is having trouble with his own game; he still gives advice. In general it's best never to accept fragmentary advice if the person giving it does not consider the whole picture and how the advice relates to your individual game. View fragmentary advice with suspicion.

4. YOUR APPROACH: THE "LINE" AND HOW TO FIND IT

A beginning bowler usually pays little attention to where he takes his stance or where the ball rolls at the arrows. He's more concerned with just bowling. Experienced bowlers, on the other hand, have found that it pays to be more precise. They know that all lanes provide certain points of reference. And over the years, they have learned to use these points to aim their shots with precision.

POINTS OF REFERENCE

All bowling lanes consist of thirty-nine parallel boards, which are "numbered" from right to left and are your main reference points (Figure 4–1). To make it easier to find a particular board, every fifth one is marked with dots and arrows. (Some houses, though, don't mark the 5- and 35- boards in the approach area.) In most houses there are two sets of dots behind the

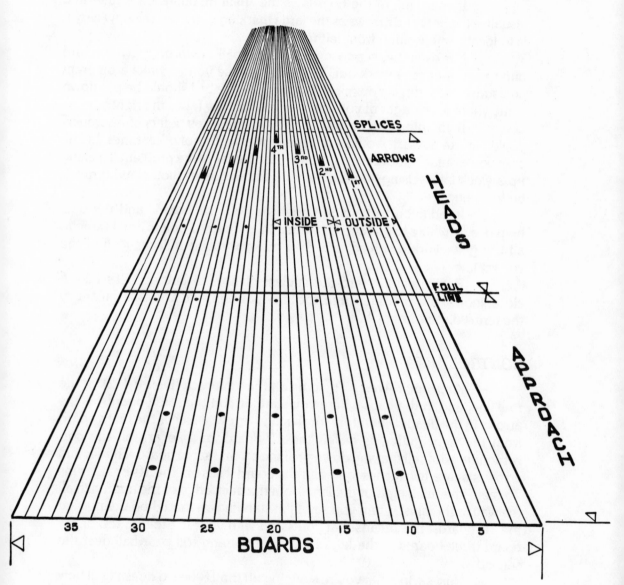

Figure 4–1   Points of reference

foul line, one at 15 feet and one at 12 feet. A third set of dots is located at the foul line and approximately sixteen feet beyond the foul line are several arrows for aiming your ball.

If you think of the boards as the small markings on a ruler and visualize the dots and arrows as the large markings, you can see how easy it is to locate any position from left to right.

For example, suppose you set the ball down on a given board and the shot doesn't work out. This might cause you to make a different adjustment next time. You might suspect that the ball should be put down somewhere to the right of your prior shot. But how far to the right?

If you didn't know how to use the boards as points of reference, you'd have to guess. It would work sometimes while not other times. In any case you wouldn't know exactly how to handle the same problem if it came up a week later Using your knowledge of the boards, you stand a much better chance.

In addition to helping target the ball, the boards and the dots help decide where to line up. Of course the reference points don't remove all the guesswork involved, but they make it much quicker to find the correct line.

Before getting into the subject of how to line up, let's take a closer look at the approach area, the back position, and at what is meant by the term "displacement."

CONTROL AREA

Approach Area / The dots on the approach (Figure 4–2), at the foul line, and in the back where you start, are on the same boards as the arrows in the heads. Therefore, the second arrow, which is the tenth board from the right gutter, is called the 10-board, and so are all the corresponding dots all the way down the lane on that same board. The second arrow is only a few inches long. But the board it sits on, the 10-board, runs 75 feet—the full length of the lane from the back edge of the approach all the way to the pins. When you say, "I'm standing on the 18-board, playing the 10-board," this means that you stand with your left toe on top of the board three boards to the left of the third dot and roll your ball over the second arrow.

Just saying that you're standing on the 18-board doesn't tell how far back from the foul line you are. This could mean that you are standing

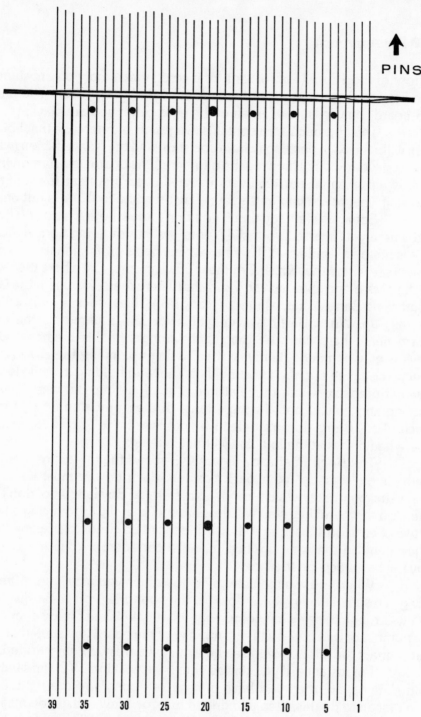

Figure 4–2   The approach area

in front of the 12-foot row of dots, or it could mean that you are standing with your heels hanging over the back edge of the approach. The phrase "18-board" only tells how far left of the right gutter you are playing.

The approach area contains two points of reference that bowlers work with: the back position (where you start) and the front position (where you finish your slide). Knowing the number of the board you start on in the back is an essential part of every expert bowler's system for lining up. Knowing what board you finish your slide on at the foul line is optional.

Some bowlers say that if you don't know both where you began and where you finished your slide, your system for lining up is deficient. This is not necessarily true. There are many good professionals who don't look to see where they finish. For these bowlers, knowing where they stand on the back of the approach and knowing where their ball rolls at the target is sufficient. Barry Asher, winner of many PBA Titles, doesn't look at where he ends up. When Barry is averaging over 230 a game for the entire tournament, there can't be too much wrong with his methods. Other bowlers may be taking plenty of time setting up, letting the crowd know how precise they are, then posting their shot and holding it, while looking down at precisely where they finished at the foul line. But when Barry is winning and they're not, the superiority of their precision doesn't mean much. Also, Barry doesn't drift in his footwork. He knows instinctively where he finishes at the foul line without looking.

The Back Position / Figure 4–3 shows the three most common methods of "sighting" your back position. Each bowler must know precisely the board on which he or she started. Bowlers who don't pay attention to where they start will float around, thereby introducing a board or two of error on subsequent shots. Under certain conditions, a one-board adjustment on the back position makes a considerable difference in the way the ball reacts on the lane.

When you want to determine how much you may have drifted on any given shot, simply glance down at the floor after you've finished your follow-through to see what board your left foot finished on. By comparing the number of that board with the number of the board you started on, you can subtract the difference to see how many boards you have drifted.

For instance, if you started your back position on 20 and finished your slide on 16, then you have moved four boards to the right. If you didn't mean to do this, then you drifted in error. However, if you meant to walk from 20 to 16, then you did what is called "walking a four-board

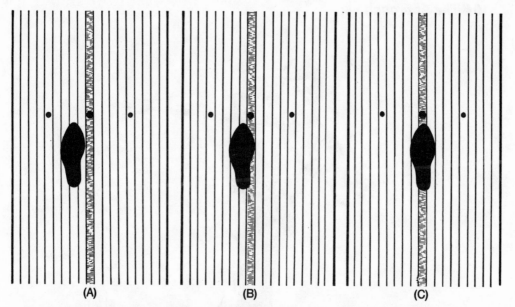

Figure 4–3   Three ways to sight your back position. (A) Letting the board show next to the instep of the left foot. (B) Closing off the board with the edge of your left foot. (C) Lining up the middle of your left shoe with the center of the board

approach line." This does not constitute an error but a line adjustment.

Displacement / Figure 4–4 shows the bowler putting the ball down on the 10-board while finishing his slide on the 16-board.

Displacement is the difference between the board you finished your slide on and the board on which you set the ball. In this illustration the bowler is delivering the ball with a six-board displacement. Sometimes this is called "shoe-to-ball-spread." The least amount of displacement normally used by experts is five boards. The radius of the ball accounts for roughly four boards of this distance. Therefore, some professionals stroke the ball by their ankle as close as the width of one board—or about one inch.

Before beginning to develop a system for lining up, it is important to know how many boards constitute your particular displacement. The easiest way to find this out is to have a friend watch where you set the ball down on each delivery. If you are practicing alone, place a white piece of paper out just beyond the foul line. Then count over from the black mark left by the ball on the paper to where you finish your slide. That difference is your displacement.

You need to know this constant when you are trying to figure out how many boards to adjust your line on any given condition.

Figure 4-4   Displacement

LINING UP YOUR APPROACH

The approach line is the imaginary line you walk to the foul line. It should NOT always follow the boards on the floor, but it should always be straight (Figure 4-5). In other words, your approach line will slant from left to right when playing deep inside (boards 15 to 20), or it may slant from right to left when playing outside (boards 7 to 1). An obvious example of walking a left-to-right slanted approach line occurs when you are trying to pick up the 10-pin.

Another reason why your approach to the foul line should be straight is that your armswing should be parallel to the line you walk. There are some outstanding bowlers who violate this rule. But don't try to prove that you're one of them, unless you have control over your game and are successful at zigzagging.

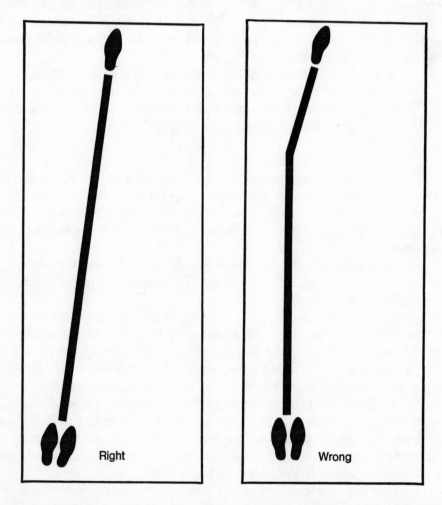

Figure 4–5   Your approach line should always be straight, regardless of the target you are using

The Line / "I found the line. . . ." This is the goal of every pro bowler in a tournament. However, when "the line" is used in discussions with beginning bowlers, it is the hardest concept to grasp and master. "The line" can be really utilized only after you have developed a sound approach and delivery. It's what every successful bowler is looking for while bowling. He works to establish it on every lane.

Throughout this book, the words "line" and "angle" are used interchangeably. This is because that is the way professionals use these terms. However, the phrase "lined up" means more. It includes having found the right angle, plus the right speed and roll. This might be better explained by inspecting the following sentences:

●*After I changed my line two boards, I had a better angle.*

●*After I changed my angle two boards, I had a better line.*

●*After I changed my angle I had a better line, but I still wasn't lined up perfectly. I needed more speed too.*

Thus, being "lined up" means:

1. You stand at the proper back position and aim at the correct target for your shot. This way, even if you miss your mark one board to the left or right, the ball still manages to get a piece of the pocket and carry a strike high or light. This situation is called "creating area"—usually a three-board area.

2. On release, the ball skids just far enough before it grabs the lane and begins its hook. It isn't sliding all the way to the pins, nor is it grabbing the lane too early.

3. The ball has the right amount of hook: neither too much arc, nor straight as a string. The ball steadies in the front of the pocket. It doesn't have the tendency to hang out to the right, leaving the 2–4–5, or jump through the "nose," leaving 4–6—this latter situation is called "high-lighting the pocket" and will be discussed in a subsequent chapter.

4. The ball hits the headpin at the best angle and speed. It is able to work its way through the pins with just the right amount of deflection and drive, keeping the pin action low to the floor, which results in maximum mixing. With the right line, you can miss your speed slightly and still carry strikes either high or light on the headpin.

Low-average bowlers rarely line up properly. They spend the entire evening fighting the lanes and then walk out blaming their poor scoring on a lack of practice. A better background in bowling theory could help solve their problem. An undeniable fact is that a bowler who is lined up will carry more "Brooklyn" and "nose" hits than a bowler who isn't lined up. Being lined up perfectly increases your "lucky" hits.

THE PARALLEL-LINE SYSTEM

Most professionals use some variation of what's called the parallel-line system when they line up. The system involves two parallel lines: your approach line and the target line (Figure 4–6).

The target line is an imaginary line drawn from the foul line to the target (spot, arrow, or board) that you have selected. Because the target is located in the "heads" area of the lane (16 feet past the foul line), some bowlers use the term "head line." However, we will usually refer to this as a "target line."

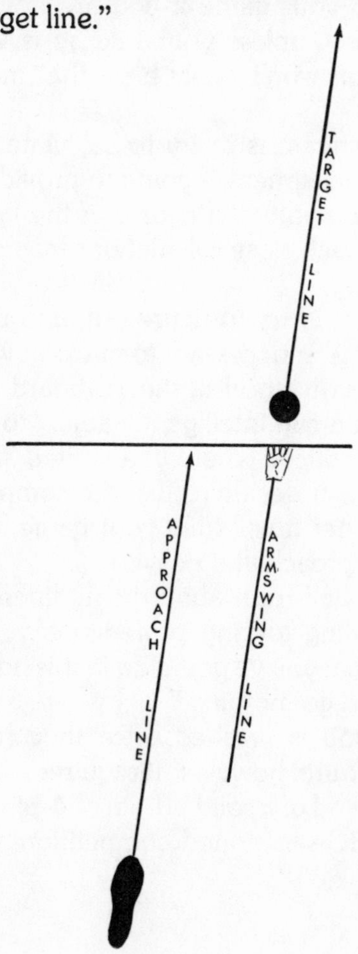

Figure 4–6   Parallel lines. If you use the parallel-lines system in adjusting your floor position, then the approach line is always parallel to the head line (target line). Also, the target line is a continuation of the armswing line. This is true no matter what angle you play

To use this system, simply make sure that your approach line is always parallel to your target line when adjusting your floor position. This means that a straight line drawn through your back position and your front position will be parallel to a line drawn through the point where the ball is placed on the lane and the target, sixteen feet past the foul line.

In reality, though, only a few pros use this entire system of matching up all four points. Those who use it often, do so only when they are having trouble. Most top bowlers pay attention only to their back position and target (where they stand and where they aim). And for many bowlers this abbreviated version works very well.

There are some strong advocates of using the full system all the time, but I don't recommend it until your game is further along. It would be absurd to bring this much precision into your game if you are not yet capable of producing accurate shots. Also, unless your release is very consistent, this kind of approach precision won't really have that much effect on the action of the ball on the pins.

Even at the expert level it is dangerous to try to calculate the exact amount of hooking power a given adjustment is going to provide— especially when the lanes are uneven and spotty. Of course, if the lanes have been playing even on all parts, then such close calculations may give satisfactory results.

In summary, even beginners should try to figure out, and then use, specific back positions and targets. It is unnecessary to guess at what back position and what target to play. If you stood at the 16-board and your shot went slightly to the left, then you can intelligently adjust to the 17-board or 18-board. But if you hadn't noticed where you started, then you couldn't adjust accurately. Whether you decide to use the complete parallel lines system depends upon whether it will help your game, and whether you're precise enough in your approach and delivery.

Incidentally, there is a popular half-truth about being lined up that is believed by many bowlers, including touring professionals. It is illustrated by this remark: "I don't know what you've got to do in this house to carry. I murdered the pocket all day and got nothing."

Many bowlers feel that their job is finished once they have "wired-in" the pocket. This is far from the truth, however. It requires a high degree of sophisticated lane-reading to get rid of a solid 10-pin or 4-pin, on both lanes, in two or three shots. (In ABC-sanctioned competition, you bowl on each lane every other frame.) That's all the time a bowler has before he reaches the middle of each game.

This subtle adjustment is the whole ball game when making a living on the professional tour. You must learn how to change the angle at the pocket and the deflection factor in order to trip the 4- and 10-pin, and carry the wall shots.

If there is a single factor which determines whether you move on to the last level in reading lanes—and a living on the tour, it is knowing how to make this final, tiny, but precise adjustment *quickly*.

At the very top in all professional sports, the difference between success and failure is microscopic. It may be: a pawn in chess; a hundredth of a second in racing; a club-face adjustment of 2 degrees in golf; or a fraction of an inch in bowling. The successful bowler makes this minute adjustment before his opponents and wins.

A SELECTION OF APPROACH LINES

Good bowlers use different approach lines to solve different lane conditions. It is impossible to list all the different approaches you might use. But here are a few that you'll find most helpful.

Right to Left / This approach line (Figure 4–7) is used when you are selecting a line that enters the pocket from an outside angle—known as "pointing the shot up." Also this angle is used when the lanes are either too oily or too spotty to play a normal hooking line. This approach may have to be walked when the middle of the lane is very dry, and the outside is the only place with enough oil to get the ball skidding properly. To play this shot stand at the extreme right and walk an approach line that slants in toward the middle of the lane (from right to left). Sometimes, bowlers who arc the ball on the back end may use a straightaway approach line when playing the first arrow and get the desired result without having to "point the shot up" to the pocket. This is because they hook the back end so well.

Left to Right / This approach (Figure 4-8) is used when bellying (arcing) the ball away from the pocket (on the front half of the lane) then hooking it back toward the head pin. The approach slants to the right and is used when playing an inside angle near the third or fourth arrow. Few other approach lines are used on inside angles, since the pocket is at the 17-board.

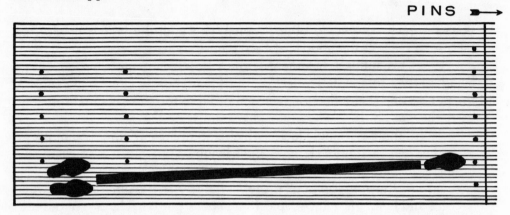

Figure 4–7   Right-to-left approach

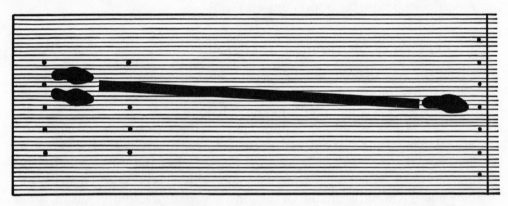

Figure 4–8   Left-to-right approach

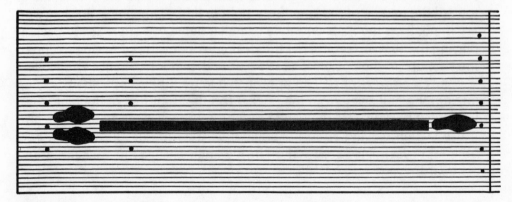

Figure 4–9   Straight approach

Straightaway / This approach line (Figure 4–9) is used when you are playing lines parallel to the boards. That is, you finish your slide on the same board that you started from. Normally, this approach line is used when your target is at or near the second arrow. Sometimes, of course, you will have to belly the ball over the second arrow on a dry lane.

Intentional Left-to-Right Slant vs. Drifting / Figure 4–10 shows an extreme left-to-right approach. Experts use this much slant only on very dry lanes. Nonetheless it represents an intentional approach line. Figure 4–11 shows unintentional drifting. When beginners drift this much, the result is reduced accuracy. Even a one-board drift may affect your accuracy enough to make the ball miss the pocket.

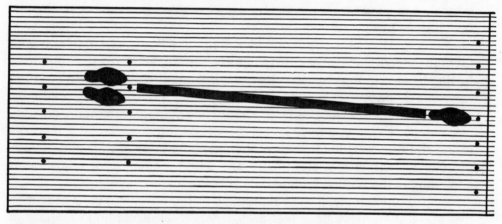

Figure 4–10   An intentionally *extreme left-to-right approach*

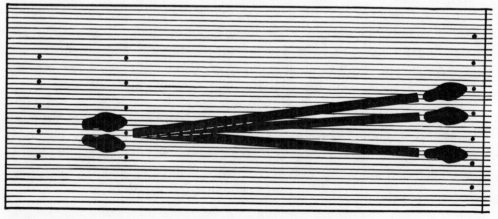

Figure 4–11   Unintentional *drifting during the approach*

SUMMARY

Some experienced bowlers have never bowled from a different back reference-point in all their years of play. But for those who do change, the following comments apply.

In playing their angles many bowlers use an inefficient, haphazard procedure that costs them untold numbers of pins. They move about wildly, trying this line and that. It's much better to use a clear, logical approach to the problem. With this in mind, here are five suggestions when bowling across a house.

1. Ask yourself: "What kind of condition am I about to bowl on?" If you've had the chance to watch others bowl, you can tell by their shots whether the condition is oily or dry. However, you must still draw definite conclusions from your own shots.

2. Begin the first game by setting up a line based either on your favorite line or best guess. Your guess should be derived either from having bowled in that house before or what you learn from practice shots.

3. Execute the line you've decided on with inner certainty, especially when throwing "search" shots while attempting to verify guesses.

4. Either you have found the line or you are searching. If you've found the line on your first shot, then execute your best. If you are still searching, then keep a clear head and begin making floor adjustments according to the basic fundamentals of lining up.

For example, if the ball hooked to the nose, and your execution was good, then move your feet and/or target left according to whatever change ratio you have decided on for this condition. (Oil requires less radical change-ratios than very dry conditions.) Moving one board at the target and one board in the back position in the same direction moves the entire line over one board. Your ability to adjust depends on your understanding of speed, loft, lift and turn, floor adjustments, angle at the pocket, and deflection of your ball. It is not easy! This is why only a few bowlers average above 190 compared to the millions under that number.

5. Move to the next pair of lanes and open with the same line that proved successful on the prior lanes. Assume that whatever has been working will continue to work on each next pair. If you were a professional competing in tournaments, you should determine in the first four frames of each game whether any problems you are having are caused by faulty execution or by the way you elected to line up for that pair of lanes.

5. LANE CONDITIONS

The lane condition affects the bowler's score more than any other single factor in the game. In fact, the more advanced the player becomes in his physical techniques, the greater the effect lane conditions have on his success. Lane conditions are a direct result of lane maintenance. Because maintenance standards vary from house to house, the bowler must constantly adjust to different lane conditions to score.

Learning to read lanes requires a great deal of experience and sensitivity. This book can help you to recognize the problems, but nothing can replace actual experience. Only experience can give you the knowledge and ability to bowl a few balls on a strange lane and then make the required adjustments to produce a good score. However, reading this book and then discussing these ideas with better bowlers is a beginning.

This chapter describes the basic components of lanes, how they are maintained, how they are oiled, and how their "condition" can affect your score.

STRUCTURE OF A DRESSED LANE

A dressed lane is made up of three parts: the wood and its surface, the finish, and an oil film. All three parts (Figure 5–1) create the "condition."

All new lanes are built to be perfectly flat. But through use, they begin to show signs of wear. Little "dings," caused by the lofted shot, begin to appear in the heads; the finish begins to wear down as balls continuously roll over it. If a new coat of finish isn't applied when needed, the wood on the right side of the alley bed will begin to wear down, creating a surface that isn't level. As a result, right-handers bowl on a lane that is different from the one the left-handers bowl on. After some time, the lanes must be resurfaced.

In resurfacing, the lane is sanded down to a level than can vary no more than 40/1000 inch, with the measurement taken from gutter to gutter. The tolerance must be checked and approved by the ABC. The lane should be resurfaced every year, or at least every other year.

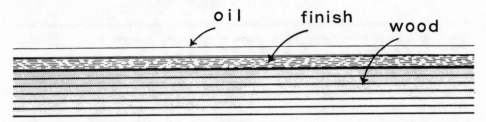

Figure 5–1   Structure of a dressed lane

RESURFACING

Figure 5–2 shows side views of three lanes. The lane at the top is the ideal lane. It is perfectly level. It has an even condition when accompanied by a proper oil application. This lane condition lasts only a few months after resurfacing.

The middle illustration shows the side view of worn or poorly resurfaced lanes. The heads still have high and low spots due to the constant impact of the ball. Microscopic depressions in the lane are caused by ball wear and poor resurfacing. The drawings are exaggerated for illustrative purposes, but a bowling ball reacts critically to slight imperfections on the lane's surface. So, even if the 40/1000 inch requirement is

Figure 5–2

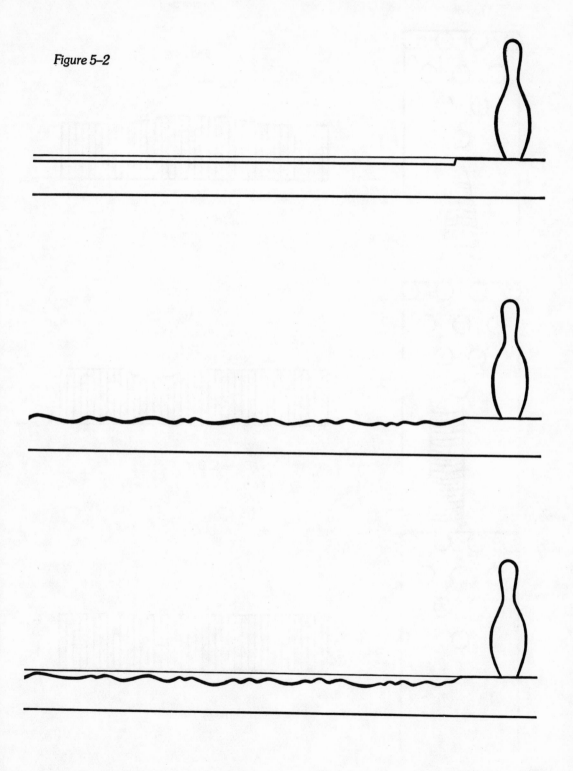

Top view

Figure 5–3

End view

"Crowned" condition

"Dished" lane

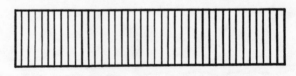

Perfectly flat

met when sanding, uneven resurfacing techniques and wear can create a poor lane condition quickly.

The bottom illustration shows a badly cut or worn lane to which coats of finish have been applied. When the coat of finish is poured on, it runs to the low spots in the lane and dries. But instead of having a flat playing surface, there still exist open-grain boards. The effect of open-grain boards will be explained in more detail later.

Let us now take a look at different resurfacing patterns. The drawing at the top of Figure 5–3 shows a "crowned" condition. This occurs when the lanes have been purposely cut down on the outsides, leaving a slight hump in the middle of the lane, say from 15-board to the 25-board. The crowned condition creates an extremely high scoring condition because the ball is allowed to roll (not slide) against the hump without crossing over into the "nose" or "Brooklyn" area of the headpin.

When the ball churns against the crown, its revolutions—or spinning force—are actually increased. As it travels down the lane, it is like a time bomb ready to explode. As soon as the crown ends, the ball is allowed to charge and explode into the pocket. It exists for both right- and left-handers, since it runs from the 15-board to the 25-board.

A crowned condition will cause the following:

1. Increased hitting power.

2. Minimum breakdown of line due to a wood "wall" that guides the hook of the ball. Normally, there is only oil to stop the hook of the ball, and it does so by making the ball skid—not roll.

3. A natural holding pattern. Then when you put an oil "wall" on top of the crown, it creates a double "wall."

A crowned condition is rare because it requires a lot of the resurfacer's time and knowledge, as well as considerable down time and lost money for the proprietor. We won't discuss the ethics involved.

The middle picture in Figure 5–3 is an example of a "dished" lane. Below are listed some of the factors associated with such resurfacing.

1. This condition is more common than authorities are willing to admit. It also causes left-handers to have an advantage over right-handers, since the left side of the lane is left flat.

2. The condition is created quickly by sanding out only that area of the lane which is most worn—from the 10-board to the 20-board on the right side. Some resurfacers say this is done

because the proprietors put time pressures on them since the lanes have to be closed while resurfacing.
3. It causes the ball to hook more than on a flat lane, but hook unevenly.
4. It causes finish to build up in the middle of the lane.
5. It creates "highlighting" (a touchy condition that will be explained later). Simply put, this causes the ball to hang out to the right or jump left. Lining up wrong causes the same reaction, so don't be too quick to fault the lane by thinking it is dished.

The bottom drawing in Figure 5–3 illustrates a perfectly level condition. It is the fairest condition. There are no high or low spots on the lane that come into play with the ball. When an even oil pattern is laid down the bowler is allowed to play his best shot and score. The ball will react evenly. There are no advantages built into any part of the lane.

Open-Grain Boards / Open-grain boards are caused by the finish wearing off, leaving the pine exposed to the heavy pounding of thousands of balls thrown down the middle and right side.

Figure 5–4a shows an open-grain board as it may appear on the lane. Figure 5–4b shows an end view of that board after it is removed from the lane. Figure 5–4c is a cross-section blow-up of a typical open-grain board. Notice how rough the surface is on the soft grain of an open-grain pine board. When you run your hand across the lane, it feels somewhat like the edges of a hair comb.

This illustration shows only one open-grain board, but in reality several develop at the same time, usually on the part of the lane where the heaviest play occurs. The lanes have to have unusual use, or be in terrible shape, for open-grain boards to appear on the left side of the lane. Open-grain boards are usually the curse of the right-handed bowler, especially when they are present in front of the pocket. They cause the ball to jump around and hook unevenly.

When lanes get in this shape, each worn board must be replaced or the lanes must be resurfaced. Unfortunately, open-grain boards commonly exist on sanctioned lanes. As long as the lanes are within legal tolerances and no pressure is brought to bear on the proprietors, these conditions will continue to hamper scoring.

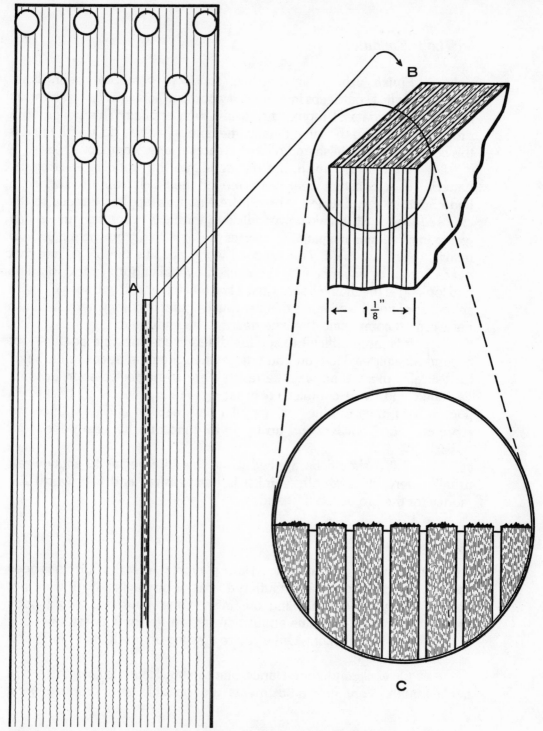

Figure 5–4   Artist's rendition of a close-up of an open-grain board. The finish has worn off and the wood has been damaged by the pounding of thousands of bowling balls. The lane should be refinished as soon as possible

Finish / After a lane has been sanded, several coats of finish are applied. The first coat seeps into the raw wood and acts as a sealer. Normally three to four coats of regular finish are then applied. This builds up a protective cover on the lane. Finally, the lane is dressed daily with oil. It is this combination of finish and oil that creates a lane "condition."

Without the finish, the oil seeps into the wood in an irregular pattern. When constant wear has removed the finish from the surface, a bad condition can develop. The oil dressing now applied directly to the exposed wood will break down quickly (normally every one and a half games in a five-man league). This causes the lanes to dry out, no matter how heavily they were oiled. The exposed wood absorbs the oil. A lane that needs a coat of finish can be recognized by walking up to the foul line and looking at the maple boards just a few feet beyond. If you see yellowish splotches of finish, and areas that are much lighter in color where the finish has worn off completely, the lane needs to be refinished.

It is more difficult to see the difference in the pine boards—out beyond the splices. How do you adjust when the pine needs refinishing? Realistically, there is no way. Lanes that are so neglected soon become damaged and need complete resurfacing. Frequently called brickyards (Figure 5–5), they produce an irregular ball reaction and are difficult to score on. Good bowlers end up trying to grind out the least poor score possible.

Finish should be applied when the lane begins to show wear, usually every three months. Finish is inexpensive, and well worth the money for the protection it provides.

OIL

It is the presence of oil that makes a lane playable. After the finish has been applied, the daily job of distributing a coat of oil begins. If oil were not present and you were bowling on finish alone, your ball would hook drastically. There's one plus about bowling on finish: It doesn't get any slower the rest of the night. Once you're bowling on finish, that's it. That is as slow as it can get.

On well-conditioned lanes, one can bowl like a jeweler instead of a blacksmith. Very fine adjustments are possible and produce great

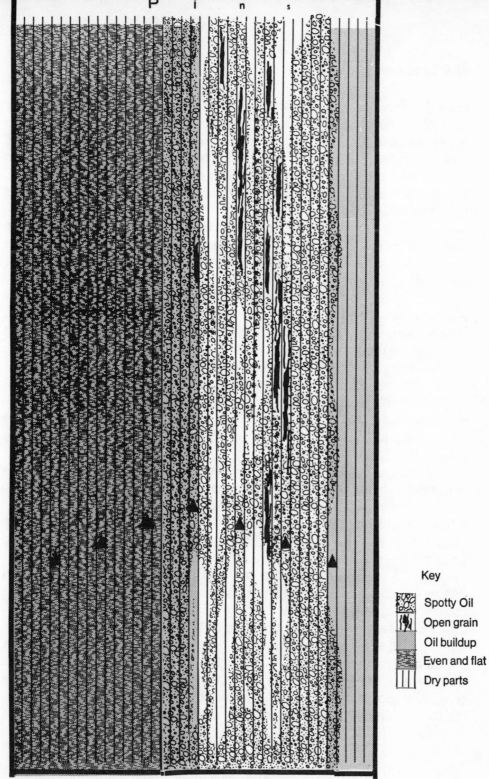

P i n s

Key

Spotty Oil

Open grain

Oil buildup

Even and flat

Dry parts

Figure 5–5   A "brickyard" is the worst condition of all

rewards. This is not possible when lanes are not kept up. Oil must be applied to the lanes daily for two reasons. Oil is a liquid and subject to evaporation. It is also moved and removed by the roll of the ball (the ball picks up the oil, causing you to wipe it off with a towel). Both evaporation and roll of the ball cause what is known as a "breakdown in condition." When this happens, you should make floor adjustments to maintain a good line, if possible.

The daily application of oil can either be made by hand and then buffed, or by machine (most of the time, it's the latter). In Figure 5–6 the dark shades of color represent the oil distribution on the lane. The darker the shading, the heavier the distribution of oil.

Lane 1 in Figure 5–6 has been oiled by hand and then buffed. It is a better way to oil a lane because the act of buffing not only cleans the lane but also forces the oil to penetrate the lane. The oil doesn't just float on top of the finish as in the case of machine oiling. This penetration allows the condition to hold up better under heavy use.

When this method is used, a lane need be oiled only once a day. However, proprietors seldom have oil applied by hand because it is more expensive than machine application. To hand-buff every lane in a house takes time and knowledge, both of which require the extra cost of a dying breed—the "lane man."

Lane 2 in Figure 5–6 has been oiled by machine. Since it is more convenient and economical, it is the method chosen by most proprietors. Because the machine allows the coat of oil to float on top of the finish, it is more subject to being moved and removed by the roll of the ball and by evaporation. For this reason, lanes done by machine may require oiling twice a day—once early in the morning and again before the late league.

There are many different types of oil. Oil can be found in different viscosities for climates of high and low humidity. Each house must choose the type of oil that is best suited to local conditions. In hot dry desert climates, for example, a heavier oil is required.

Oil application is one of the most important factors in creating a playable condition. One of the leading authorities on lane maintenance, Sam Baca of the PBA, says: "You have to have three factors present to guarantee good scores: The ball must be able to skid two-thirds of the way, roll the remaining one-third of the way, and have a change of direction [on the back end]."

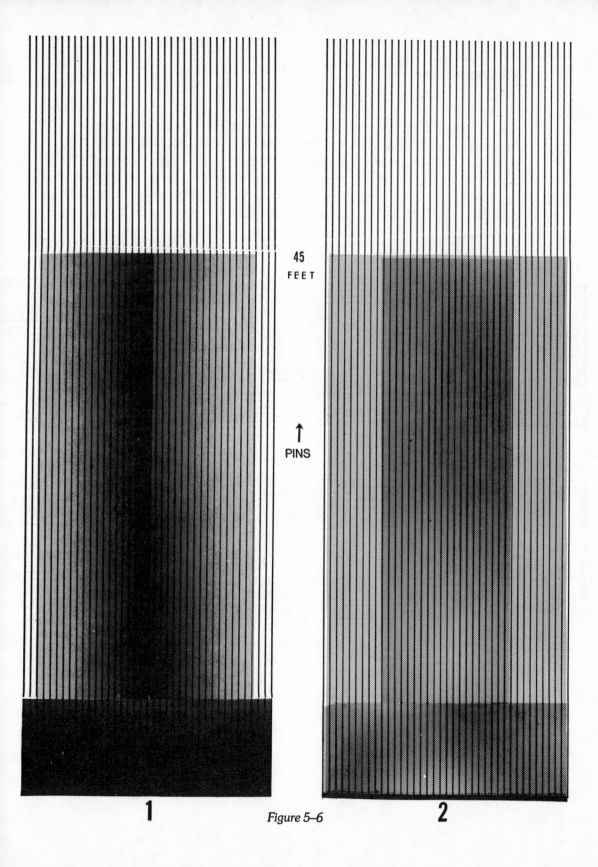

45
FEET

↑
PINS

1

Figure 5–6

2

Oil Patterns

Even Conditions / Take a look at the top drawing in Figure 5–7. If oil were visible, this is how it would appear when applied evenly from gutter to gutter and from foul line to forty-five feet. Contrary to what you might think, this method of applying oil leads to some of the worst conditions, and is thus not recommended. If you bowl on this condition while it's fresh, it's okay, but it breaks down too quickly into a spotty condition.

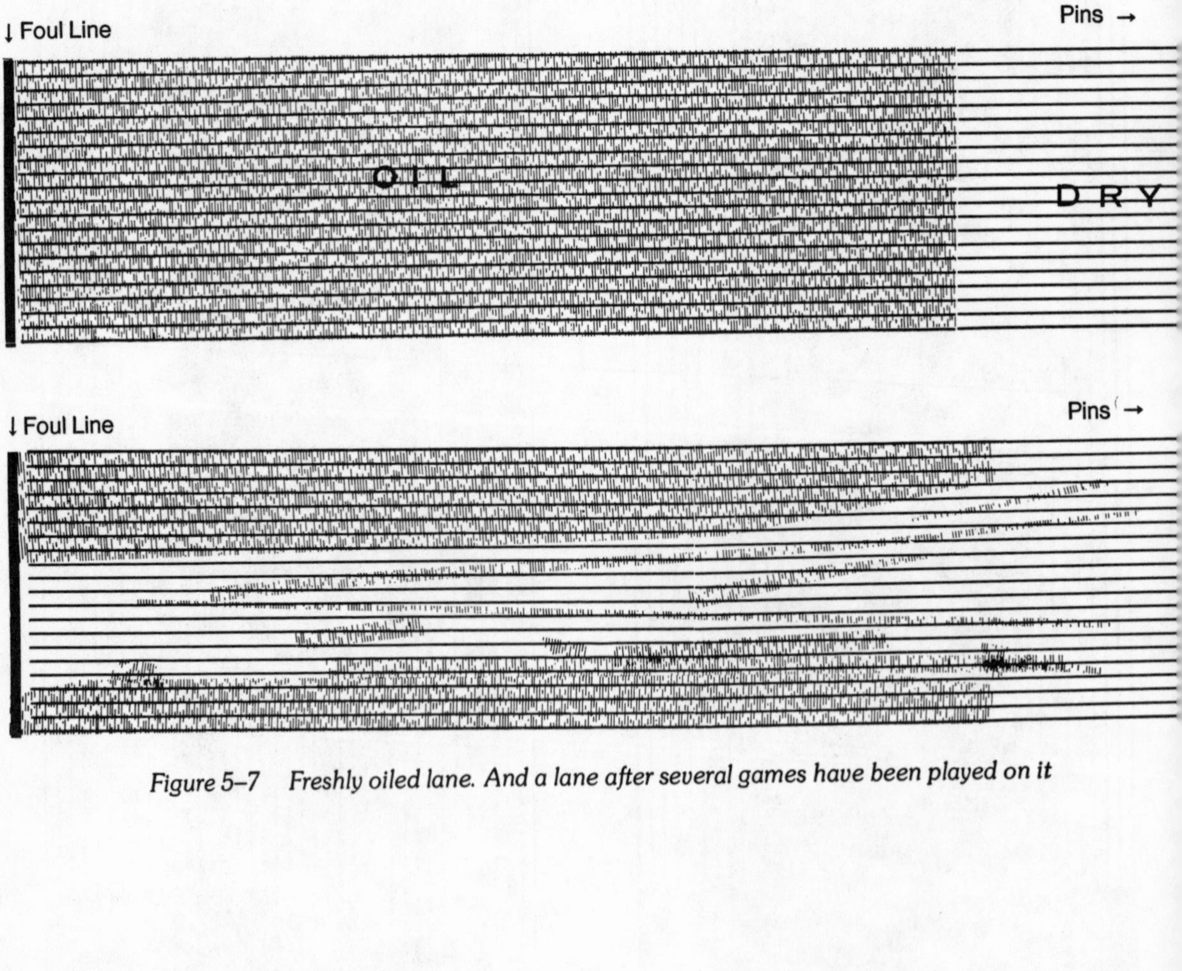

↓ Foul Line   Pins →

↓ Foul Line   Pins →

Figure 5–7   Freshly oiled lane. And a lane after several games have been played on it

Spotty Condition / The bottom drawing shows how the first lane would look after a few hours of bowling. This pattern—oil on the sides and spotty dryness in the middle—develops because most bowlers are right-handed and like to throw closer to the middle of the lane than nearer to the gutter. Thus the ball picks up oil and moves it. Later it becomes dry in the middle and slick on the sides, and is very difficult to score on. Touring pros facetiously refer to this condition as a "reverse block."

Double Oiled Heads / This pattern (shown in Figure 5–8) is generally recommended as the one with the least faults for both average and high-average bowlers. The heads are double-oiled to allow the ball to skid two-thirds of the way down the lane. The oil is applied no farther down than forty-five feet. The back ends are left dry and the outsides are lightly

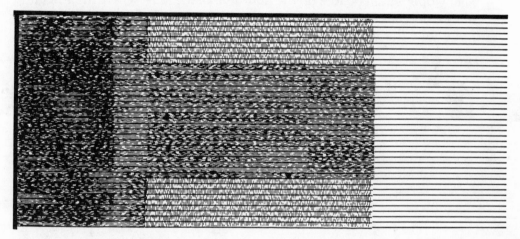

Figure 5–8   The best oiling pattern

oiled. This permits the lane to be heavily played in the middle without breaking down too quickly. It allows balls to slide yet roll (and hook) the last fifteen feet to the headpin. It enables bowlers to play more than one scoring angle, and it allows both big hookers and straight-line ball shooters to find angles for their shots.

Reverse Block Condition / This familiar condition (Figure 5–9) occurs when lane maintenance has been skipped for one day (such as on the lane maintenance man's day off, with nobody covering for him; or when a machine has broken down for a day or so; or when management is short of help or too busy or just doesn't care). It's super dry in the middle and spotty oil on the outside. If the lanes haven't been finished properly, this condition can develop in less than a day. The problem is compounded by any open-grain boards on the right side of the lane, where the soft grain in the wood has swelled up and hardened. You can feel this with your hand if you take the time to walk down the lane about two-thirds of the way.

Figure 5–9   45$'$

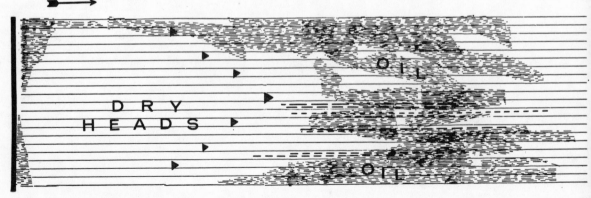

Reverse block

Dry heads—back end oily

Sometimes the lane is also like this just beyond the splices (twenty feet beyond the foul line). But it always appears on the right side, where most right handers roll their ball.

Dry Heads and Back End Spotty Condition / The dotted lines in the bottom drawing of Figure 5–9 indicates open-grain boards, the shaded parts of the lane show the oil. This is the worst of all lane maintenance foul-ups—dry heads and spotty oil on the back end, as well as open-grain boards with the finish worn off. Experts hate this condition. There is no skid. The ball grabs before it gets to the arrows, then "snakes" (hooking a little, stopping a little, hooking a little, stopping some more) on the back end. The only reason this condition is tolerated is that the general bowling public doesn't know about it and cannot complain. It will occur more commonly in houses that have not been resurfaced in over two years.

One top pro facetiously comments that the first thing he does when he goes into a strange bowling establishment is to check the cleanliness of the rest room. He says: "If the proprieter doesn't care about his rest rooms, which are inspected, he surely won't care about his lanes, since oil is invisible." There's more truth than humor in this remark.

Cross-Wipe Condition / This is a common method of distributing oil (top drawing in Figure 5–10). The middle of the lane—where the traffic is—is given a higher concentration of oil than the outside. The lanes are then cross-wiped, which fans out the oil towards the gutters. It is done the same for both sides . . . usually.

Hold Spot Condition / This condition (middle drawing, Figure 5–10) can be created on both sides of the lane. Sometimes, however, it is done only on the right side (when the finish is not holding the oil) in an effort to even the sides and bring the scoring into balance. It is possible to delay the breakdown on the heavier-used right side of the lane by putting a concentration of oil in the right track (as shown in the illustration). Another problem develops, however, when it gets a little "too good" at holding the ball on line.

Full Wet Block Condition / This pattern (bottom drawing, Figure 5–10) also creates high scores except that you won't get as much help from the lane if you "belly" the ball. This is because the outsides are lightly oiled while the middle still has the "wall" all the way to the pocket. Lanesmen who "doctor" lanes in this manner often create an unequal scoring condition when the right side breaks down while the left side stays up, because ball-wear causes the finish to absorb the oil unevenly. This unintentional foul-up frequently causes a left-hand versus right-hand controversy.

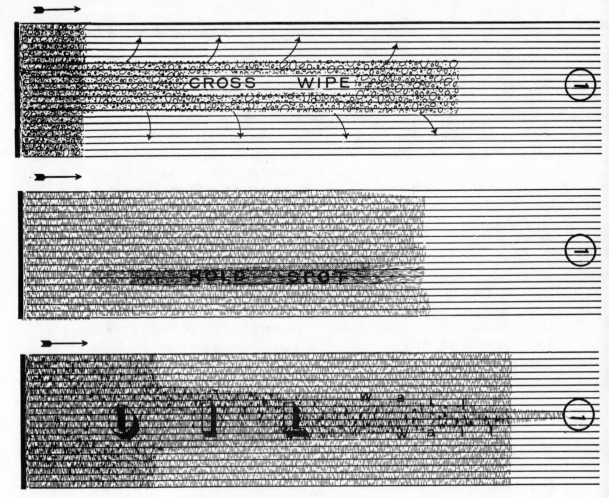

Figure 5–10   A full wet block, one of several possible "blocked" lane conditions. Note: the wall of oil in the center of the lane

Full (Wet-Dry) Block Condition / The primary reason for creating this condition (Figure 5–11) is to inflate scores. However, if the bowler doesn't know how to line up, to make use of the "wall," his scoring can actually become lower and erratic. The outsides of the lane are left dry so the ball will grab and hook back to the headpin. Then a heavy oil "wall" is laid down in the middle to prevent the ball from hooking farther left of the pocket. When this "wall" extends all the way to the pocket, it is called a "full" block. It can produce the highest "intentional" scoring condition.

Short (Wet-Dry) Block Condition / This pattern is created for the same reasons as a full wet-dry block. The difference is that the heavy

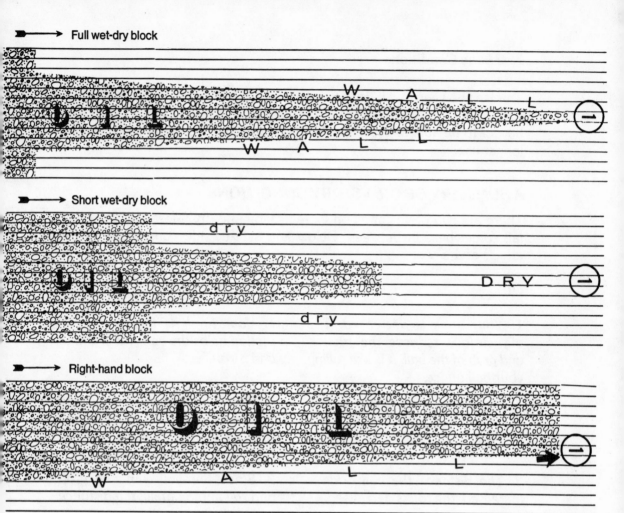

Figure 5–11   Oil conditions—intentional patterns

concentration of oil (wall) in the middle does not extend all the way to the headpin. It ends anywhere from 35 to 45 feet from the foul line, and allows the ball to hook left into the nose and Brooklyn when you don't play the correct angle. But if you do know how to line up on this condition you can shoot "telephone numbers."

    Right-hander's Blocked Condition / When the ride side of a lane becomes so unevenly tracked that right-handers cannot compete with scores coming off the left side, a blocked condition has been used as a "quick and dirty" answer. There is little satisfaction in a 240 game knowing that *every* missed shot was caught by the "wall" and converted into a strike.

This isn't bowling and it isn't fair, especially to left-handers. The ABC Rules state clearly that these methods are illegal. But it is wise for even a novice bowler to be able to recognize blocked-lane conditions (until they are no longer used).

A SUMMARY OF OIL VS. DRY CONDITIONS

There are two basic condition extremes: oil and dry. Most conditions will fall somewhere in between. Below is a side-by-side comparison of the effects of the two:

OIL	*DRY*
1. Your hook is decreased. The oily surface reduces the friction and grab of the ball. It is like rolling your ball on ice.	*1. Your hook is increased. The friction helps the ball grab the lane and turn.*
2. Ball speed is increased due to more skid and less friction.	*2. Because of greater friction, the ball rolls more, skids less, and ball speed is decreased (requiring you to throw with more speed).*
3. The distance the ball skids is increased; the roll is decreased.	*3. Since the ball wants to grab and roll immediately, the distance it skids is decreased.*
4. More ball deflection at the pocket, less drive.	*4. More drive, less ball deflection at the pocket.*
5. On a normal entry angle, the ball will tend to have more light-pocket hits and pocket splits (5–7, 8–10, 5–10).	*5. Your normal shot will result in more high-pocket hits, and nose splits (4–6, 6–7, 7–10, 4–10).*

6. YOUR PINS ARE TALKING

All bowlers should be able to read pins. Watching which pins go down, how they fall, and which remain standing can give you a world of information about what you're doing wrong and how to correct it. Yet few bowlers are aware of this.

If they watch their pins at all, the chances are that most people don't know how to read them correctly. Or, to put it another way, their pins are constantly "talking" to them, but they have yet to learn the language.

And that's not all. Many people have misconceptions about pins and how they react. For example, a lot of people believe that "pins literally fly over the top of each other." This is simply not true. Pins twelve inches apart don't have enough room to climb that fast. (However, some light-weight pins will climb above the belly to the narrow neck.)

Another misconception is that pin action is impossible to explain because it is random and capricious: "Pins just go every which way imaginable." This notion is also not true. Pin action is subject to laws of physics. With a slow-motion camera, you can determine the reasons for pin action in every type of hit. But, better than that, a sharp-eyed expert can "see" everything happening in the pocket as he bowls. It is a matter of understanding pin theory and looking at live pin action for a few years. However, many bowlers have watched pin action for years and still have not *seen* the detail and what it means. A third misconception is that "if two pins weigh the same, their pin action will also be the same." This was true in the past, but it is no longer true. Two pins with identical total weights may follow the same direction. But, because of different centers of gravity, one flies higher coming off the wall, causing the carry power for pocket hits to vary dramatically. Everything else being equal, a bowler averaging six to seven strikes per game can have his strike average fall to two or three strikes per game with a change of pin type.

Touring pros develop such a quick, discriminating eye that they are able to stand on the concourse and, by watching and listening to the pin action, tell you the approximate weight of the pin, and whether the pins are "flyers" or not. "Flyers" are pins that have had some weight taken out of their bottoms, below their normal centers of gravity. This raises the center of gravity and causes them to topple more easily (some say at a seven-degree tilt; in the past a ten degree tilt was needed). Unfortunately, this type of pin construction has had an undesirable effect on bowlers who have trained themselves to throw a strong ball.

Before flyers were manufactured, the pins stayed closer to the floor, especially as they came off the wall. With wall action taking place in about 80 percent of the first balls thrown, you can see that flyers tend to defeat their own purpose, particularly for bowlers who throw a powerful shot. The pins now tend to "climb" too high on the wall, passing the corner pins belly to neck rather than belly to belly. Flyers carry well for bowlers who just roll the ball down the lane end over end.

READING THE PINS

If you want to read lanes correctly, you must learn to interpret pin action. Bowlers who understand pin action use this knowledge to change their angles. By carefully noting which pins topple and which pins remain, a bowler can determine which direction he should move his line. (For example, you may hear a pro bowler say: "I was too deep with my feet and was leaving the five-pin or seven-pin on wall shots, so I tightened up my line a couple of boards in the back and started packing the pocket." Or: "I was coming up high on the headpin and leaving 4-pins, so I loosened my line two boards in the back and started tripping the 4-pin."

If you put professional bowlers on shadow practice (without pins), they can establish a line to the pocket, but they need the pins to complete their final adjustments regarding carry power.

Because the pins are arranged in the same symmetrical pattern, you always know how they will react to a certain kind of hit. As a result, if your first ball leaves a baby split (the 3–10), you know that it hit the headpin in a certain, incorrect way. If it leaves a 2–4–5 spare, you know that it hit the headpin in a different—but also incorrect—way.

If you know how to interpret this kind of information, you can get a pretty good idea of what is going wrong. And, most important, you can make adjustments to correct the problem.

To read pin fall correctly, you must know the effect of the ball on the headpin, and the way pins are deflected into each other.

HEADPIN IMPACT POINTS AND ZONES

The face of the headpin can be marked off into many contact points (Figure 6-1). The actual point at which the ball hits the headpin is called the "impact point."

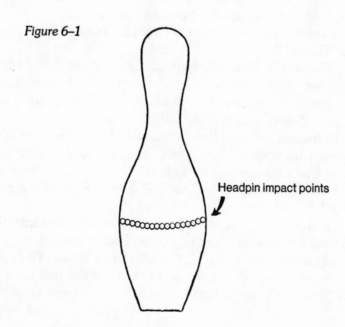

Figure 6–1

Headpin impact points

All the theoretical impact points on the headpin are not significant in themselves, but they become important in interpreting pin action when they are grouped into zones.

As the bowler begins associating specific groups of spare leaves with certain parts of the headpin, and as he associates certain kinds of strikes or splits with other parts of the headpin, he will be on his way to understanding pin action. When he can relate these observations to changes in floor position, release, or speed, he is on his way to reading lanes.

Step one is recognizing how impact points on the headpin relate directly to pin action and leaves. Step two is determining how to adjust your line by your reading of the impact point and the specific pin action.

An expert bowler can interpret the pin action of other bowlers as well as his own. This is how pros are able to get clues on where to start playing the lanes, without having to throw a ball.

We know that the ball can hit the headpin anywhere from extreme right (bucket) to extreme left (Brooklyn). For purposes of this analysis, we will break this area down into four "zones"—called "bucket," "pocket," "nose," and "Brooklyn." The "pocket" is the most important zone, and it is further divided into subzones. It is possible, of course, to analyze the other three zones—it just isn't beneficial.

Bucket / The zone farthest right on the headpin (Figure 6–2) is called the "Bucket."

When the ball hits this farthest-right zone of the headpin, either a "dinner bucket" (2–4–5–8) is left or a portion of it, perhaps just the 2-pin. Other combinations that can be left when you hit the bucket on the right are: 2–7, 2–8, 2–4–5, and 2–4–5–7–8.

In these cases the headpin is sliced so thinly by the ball that it always passes in front of the 2-pin, leaving the 2-pin and other pins standing. The headpin can be hit so thinly that it doesn't even take out the 7-pin off the wall; this leaves the "half" (2–4–5–7–8)—still a variation of the "bucket hit."

Pocket / The pocket is that zone on the headpin that causes more frustration to bowlers than any other. Even a perfect angle to this part of the headpin may not carry all ten pins for a strike. The cause of this "mystery" is the amount of deflection and drive the ball has through the rest of the pins. If the ball deflects too much, weak spares will be left—like

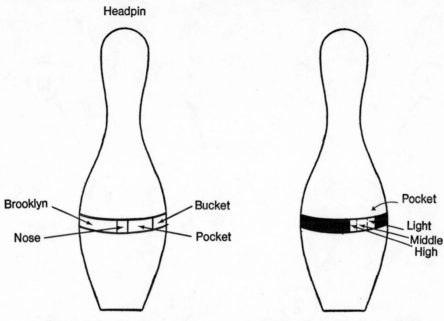

Headpin

Brooklyn —   — Bucket

Nose —   — Pocket

Figure 6–2   Headpin zones

— Pocket

Light
Middle
High

Figure 6–3   Pocket subzones

the 8-pin, 10-pin (or both), or the 5–7. If the ball doesn't deflect enough, it will leave a "strong angle" spare like the 9-pin.

Pocket Subzones / The pocket zone itself can be divided into three subzones (Figure 6–3): high, middle, and light. Hitting the headpin in any of these subzones produces a different effect.

Corner Pins / By hitting the right—or light—side of the pocket, the 7-pin spare is left. The 4-pin spare is left by a high—or left-side—pocket hit. Somtimes a 10-pin spare is left when hitting the middle-pocket. Advanced bowlers pay close attention to which subzone their ball hits. Most of them, when perfectly lined up, can play for the light- or high-pocket hit. Likewise, they can set up their line for a middle-pocket "packed" shot. This degree of accuracy on the professional-tour level is not uncommon.

Nose / The nose zone of the headpin is located directly at the midpoint. It covers an area of about an inch. When the headpin starts missing the 2-pin to the right, but doesn't hit the right side of the 5-pin, the cause is a nose hit. Hitting the headpin on the nose usually results in the following pin leaves: 7–10, 4–6, 4–6–7–10, 4–6–7, 4–7–10, 6–7–10, 6–7, 4–10, etc. The point is that hitting the nose sometimes results in two or more pins being left to form a split. Unfortunately, one of the pins is on one side of the vacant 5-pin spot while the other pin(s) are on the other side.

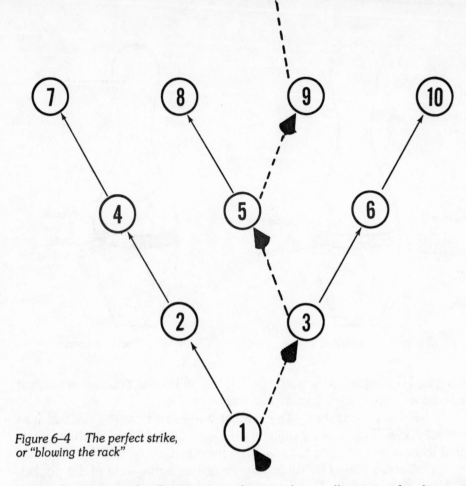

Figure 6–4   *The perfect strike,*
or "blowing the rack"

When the pins are this far apart, professionals usually just go for the count, instead of trying to pick up a spare.

Brooklyn / This is the largest zone and the least interesting to analyze. It starts just slightly to the left of center and extends all the way to the extreme left side of the headpin. In a Brooklyn-type hit, the headpin takes the 5-pin out by hitting the 5-pin on its right side.

Most advanced bowlers feel that when they have missed their target badly to the left, their error is obvious. They have pulled the shot inside their target line or let up on the speed.

THE PERFECT STRIKE

Also called "blowing the rack," or the "packed" strike (Figure 6-4), it is one of two pocket strikes that require no side-wall action. The perfect strike

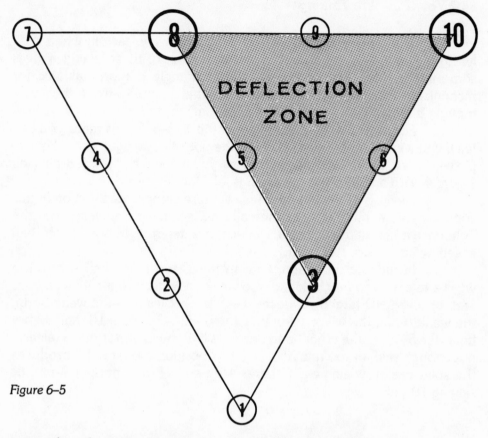

Figure 6–5

occurs less than 10 percent of the time—when the ball hits the 1-, 3-, 5-, and 9-pins.

More commonly, in the middle-pocket hit, the 3-pin takes out the 6-pin, then stays in front of the ball and takes out the 9-pin as well. Thus, in most middle-pocket strikes the ball actually hits only three pins (1, 3, and 5). The rest of the pins are taken out by pin action.

DEFLECTION ZONE

The average bowler sees the pins as a large triangle. But to interpret pin action, you must observe two triangles: the outer one with the 1-, 7-, and 10-pins at its corners; and the inner one with the 3-, 8-, and 10-pins at its corners. This inner triangle (Figure 6–5) is called the "deflection zone."

The bowler should be concerned with two factors when analyzing pin action—location and deflection. Each of these triangles gives some information about both. The outer triangle is more valuable for recognizing location—where the ball hit the headpin—while the inner triangle is more helpful in reading deflection.

For example, by watching how the 1–2–4–7 pins react, you can tell if you were too high or too light in the pocket. Too light, and a light 7-pin will be left. Or on dry lanes with flyers, you will leave a "solid" 8-pin (see Figure 4–7). Too high, and the 4-pin is left standing.

Analysis of the inner triangle is more complicated. Action in this zone is determined mainly by the ball's deflection—its movement to the right once it has hit the headpin. Deflection is determined primarily by ball speed, release, skid, and angle.

In judging deflection, bear in mind: too much ball speed, too weak a release, too much skid, or too weak an angle (too far left with your feet, or feet AND target) produces weak pocket leaves—the weak 5-pin, the weak 8-pin, the weak 10-pin; or the 5–8, 5–10, 5–8–10, and sometimes the 5–7. On the other hand, too little ball speed, too strong a release, not enough skid, or too much angle (floor position too far right) produces the solid back-row single-pin spares—the solid 8-pin, packed 9-pin, or ringing 10-pin.

PIN DEFLECTION ROUTES

The foregoing analysis might cause one to think that anything less than perfection won't result in a strike. Of course this isn't true. Most strikes aren't perfect "packed" strikes. The pins can be deflected in a number of ways to create strikes. But here, I'll discuss only the action of the 1-, 3-, and 5-pins. These pins are most important because on pocket hits the ball comes into contact with each sequentially, and you control the ball!

1-Pin / After the ball hits the pocket, there are several deflection routes (Figure 6–6) created for the left string of pins 1–2–4–7. However, the headpin can hit the 2-pin by three main routes. It can glance off the front; it can hit the 2-pin squarely (creating a domino effect 1–2–4–7); and it can slice inside to the right (throwing the 2-pin against the left wall). Here are the three routes in detail:

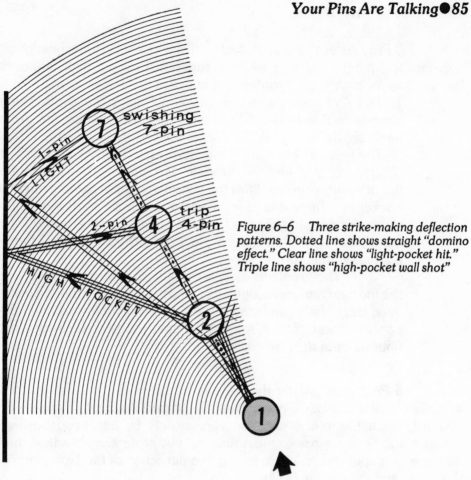

Figure 6–6   Three strike-making deflection patterns. Dotted line shows straight "domino effect." Clear line shows "light-pocket hit." Triple line shows "high-pocket wall shot"

1. On a light-pocket hit, the headpin glances off the face of the 2-pin, then ricochets off the left wall and takes out the 7-pin for a swishing 7-pin strike. It also can come off the wall on light-pocket hits and take out both the 4-pin and 7-pin by spinning off the 4-pin for a "light-pocket wall shot."

2. On a middle-pocket hit, the headpin starts the 2-pin straight down the 1–2–4–7 line, creating a domino effect.

3. On a high-pocket hit, the headpin glances off the inside or right side of the 2-pin. This time it is the 2-pin that goes to the wall. After the 2-pin ricochets off the wall it takes out the 4-pin and the 7-pin for the "high-pocket wall shots."

3-Pin / After the ball deflects off the pocket of the headpin it impacts the 3-pin (Figure 6–7), which in turn hits the 6-pin. This sequence leads to two main deflection routes for the 6-pin:

1. The first route is a domino effect, with the 6-pin going straight back into the 10-pin when the ball impacts the 3-pin perfectly, as on the middle pocket packed shot (3–6–10).

2. The second deflection route carries the 6-pin into the wall at different angles and at different elevations. The illustration intentionally oversimplifies the action of a 6-pin coming out of a pocket hit. There are at least half a dozen different deflection routes for a 6-pin going to the wall. However, an expert bowler mainly wants to know if the 6-pin tripped the 10-pin, or if the 6-pin missed the 10-pin.

The problems associated with the "inner triangle" are the most difficult to recognize of all carry problems that a bowler must face. The 6-pin is the key pin when trying to carry middle-pocket strikes. The resolution of this problem separates the finalists from the non-cashers.

5-Pin / Finally, after the ball has hit the pocket on the headpin, and glanced off the 3-pin, it may or may not impact the 5-pin (Figure 6–8). The action on this pin is watched very closely by advanced bowlers. It may come as a surprise to most readers, but professionals adjust their line (speed, angle, and roll) to match up the pin action of the 1-pin, then of the 3-pin, and then of the 5-pin.

There are five main deflection routes that a 5-pin will follow as a result of a pocket hit on the headpin. However, only the three routes that may result in strikes are shown here. The 5-pin may take out the 7-pin— this is called a "ripper." The 5-pin may take out the 8-pin—called a "packed shot." The 5-pin may be missed by the ball entirely, but it still may be taken out by the wall action started by the headpin on a half-pocket hit—called a "wall shot."

Ripper and Wall Shot / When the 5-pin takes out the 7-pin for a "ripper," it is the farthest left (Figure 6–9) the 5-pin can travel and still result in a strike.

When the 5-pin stays on its spot, because the ball missed impacting it, and instead is taken out by the left-wall action started by the headpin, then this "wall shot" represents the farthest-right pin action that the 5-pin can be involved in for pocket hits.

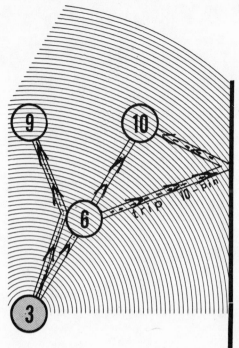

Figure 6–7   Two possible deflection routes for the 3-pin off pocket hits

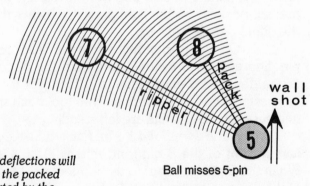

Ball misses 5-pin

Figure 6–8   Only three 5-pin deflections will produce a strike: the ripper-7, the packed shot-8, or wall-shot action started by the headpin

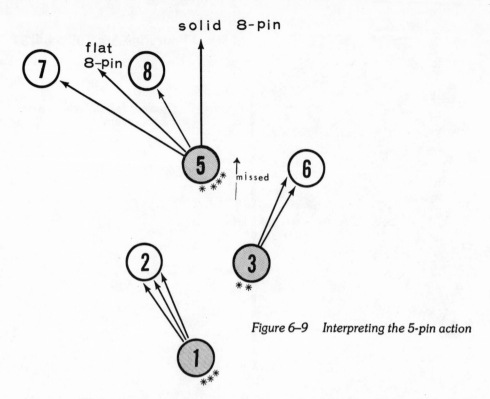

solid 8-pin

flat 8-pin

missed

Figure 6–9   Interpreting the 5-pin action

The ball hits the same part of the headpin (within the middle-pocket zone), for both the ripper and the wall shot. It is called the "half-pocket" hit, and is located in the right half of the middle-pocket zone. (If we divide the middle pocket into two halves, it is the right half. Don't confuse the half-pocket with the light pocket, which is the subzone immediately to the right.) See Figure 6–3.

On half-pocket hits, when the ball is rolling, driving left off the 3-pin, and gets back to the 5-pin, then the ripper action takes place. This action does not always result in strikes. For instance, if the same pocket-hits occur when a ball is thrown with too much speed, then the carry power decreases and 5–7 splits are left standing.

Flat 8-Pin, Solid 8-Pin, Packed Strike / When the 5-pin goes out just in front of the 8-pin (and misses it), this is known as a "flat 8-pin." When the 5-pin goes out to the immediate right (sometimes belly to neck) of the 8-pin, it is called a "solid 8-pin." When the 5-pin takes out the 8-pin perfectly (in line with the 3–5–8), it is a "packed strike."

Flat 8-pins, solid 8-pins, and packed strikes all occur after the ball hits the headpin at the same impact point at the pocket. It is the differing amount of deflection as the ball moves through the pins that causes a solid 8-pin spare or a solid strike. This common impact point is the exact place on the headpin that causes the domino effect for the 1–2–4–7.

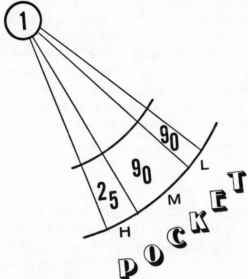

Figure 6–10   Pocket percentages

POCKET PERCENTAGES

When an expert bowler is lining up, he watches the percentage of carry on all three parts of the pocket (Figure 6–10)—high, middle, and light. He may be hitting the pocket every time, but if his carry is lower than 50 percent on all three parts of the pocket, he will not score well with that lineup.

The goal in lining up is to get maximum carry power on all three parts of the pocket—high, middle, and light. However, sometimes the best line will have good carry in only two parts of the pocket, while the third part exhibits a low percentage of carry. Pros will settle for this and often shoot a 700 series by keeping away from the low-percentage part of the pocket.

Figure 6–10 shows the carry on the high pocket to be 25 percent, while the middle and light pockets are carrying over 90 percent of the hits. If you've surmised that this happens on dry lanes, or for a bowler who can really hook the ball, then you are beginning to grasp bowling theory well. The increased hook that's usually created by a dry condition will bring the ball up to the 5-pin on half-pocket hits.

On oil, the percentage usually shifts to the left. That is, high-pocket carry goes up to 90 percent, while light- and half-pocket percentage (for rippers and wall-shots) goes down.

Percentages for the packed shot and the middle-pocket late 10-pin (trip 10-pin) usually will be high on both oily and dry conditions. Failure to get the 10-pin with a middle-pocket hit, on either oily or dry conditions, after you are lined up and have been carrying the 10-pin previously, is usually attributable to a slight increase in ball speed. Or you started bellying the ball a little bit, causing the ball to "circle" behind the headpin and front the 3-pin too much. This in turn causes the 3-pin to slice to the left of the 6-pin, throwing the 6-pin to the wall and missing the 10-pin entirely.

When your lineup is so good that every part of the pocket is carrying a high percentage of strikes, then carry on off-hits (the nose and Brooklyn) will be good, too.

SUMMARY

In this chapter, we've talked about pin action on pocket hits. This is because being able to interpret pin action on pocket hits is one of the most critical skills in bowling, particularly as you become more accurate. When your pocket hits aren't carrying, the pin action gives you the best clues as to how to adjust your line.

A firm grasp of the material in this chapter, plus careful observation of pin fall, whether you're practicing or bowling in competition, is necessary. Many otherwise good bowlers turn their minds off once the release is made. By watching pin action and interpreting it, the bowler will begin to build a foundation for reading lanes and becoming an advanced bowler.

7. LINING UP

Now that you're familiar with the different lane conditions and the problems they can cause, the next step is to learn how to minimize their effect on your score.

There are five ways to make adjustments. You can change your:

1. *Floor positions (approach line and target line)*
2. *Release*
3. *Ball speed*
4. *Style (not recommended, since even the pros don't do this very well)*
5. *Ball*

FLOOR POSITION

This is the easiest adjustment to make, the one preferred by most experts (Figure 7–1). It's the adjustment beginners should learn early, because it doesn't require changing your approach and delivery in any way. All that is required is to stand at a different starting point and/or throw at a different target.

Let's take an example to illustrate this idea.

Assume you have lined up on the approach, standing on the 16-board in the back, while finishing at the foul line on that same board (an approach line of 16 to 16). Also, you are playing a 10-to-10 target line. To adjust to lanes that are drying out during the tournament, you might try moving your back position to the left a board or two, while leaving your target the same.

If the ball still hooks into the nose, then try moving the entire line left. That is, move the back position left several boards, and move the target left at the same time. Don't forget to begin walking an approach line that slants from left to right This logic remains the same for most inside angles.

A final word, and a reminder: If you wire into the pocket, and achieve good carrying power, be prepared to make a change later on. As the oil dries up, you might have to adjust your line a little to the left. Don't assume that the line will stay the same.

RELEASE

Release changes are a little harder to accomplish successfully than floor position changes. You're getting away from what feels most comfortable to you, and thus more concentration is required to execute properly. Go to a release change only when the floor position change is not sufficient to create the best ball pattern, or when the ball hooks too early regardless of floor changes.

On a dry condition, the idea is to kill the hook enough to create better accuracy and deflection. Keeping your hand behind the ball longer than usual produces more forward roll and less spin. This causes the ball track to appear nearer the thumb hole than it usually does, thus helping to control the hook and to give better accuracy.

A few bowlers combat slow (dry) lane conditions by overturning the ball—rotating the ball so much that it skids a long way before it gets into a roll. This is not recommended. It is called "fanning the shot," and requires a high degree of wrist coordination, control, and correct analysis of lane condition.

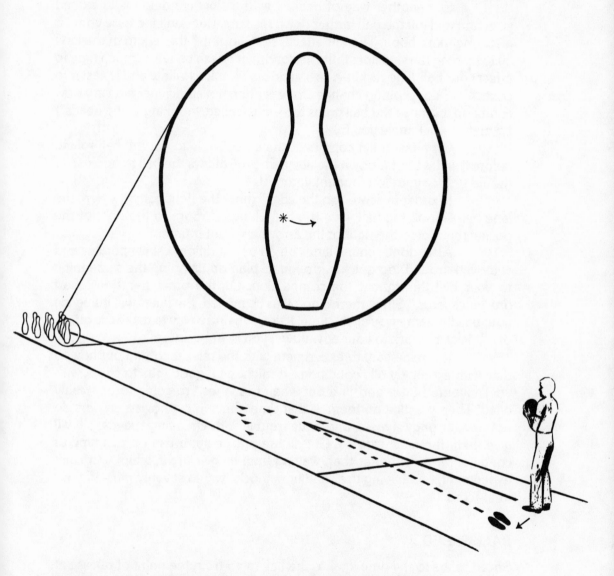

*Figure 7–1   This drawing illustrates the basic idea behind all angle or line changes.
In most cases, you should always move your feet in the direction of your problem.
Here, the ball has been hitting the headpin too far to the left, so the bowler moves
his feet to the left before the next shot. This will move headpin impact point to the right*

Still another way of dealing with a slow condition is to extend your arm and loft the ball farther down the lane. But don't increase your lift also, else more hook. The loft effectively "shortens" the length of the lane by extending the skid line; thus the condition doesn't have as much time to affect your ball. The result—the ball doesn't hook as wildly and is easier to control. A floor position change alone is often not sufficient on a very slow condition, because the ball grabs too early (called "hooking in the heads") no matter what angle you try.

On a fast (oily) condition, the objective is to get the ball rolling before it slides too far down the alley. The roll allows the ball to hook. You should reduce your loft (but not your lift).

In order to score "on the edge" (near the right gutter), where the lane helps hook the ball, give the ball plenty of room to the right of the pocket (but not to the right of the arrow, else gutter time).

Also, don't "chart" lanes on an oil condition. Oil evaporates and is moved around too quickly for you to plan on its doing the same thing to your ball throughout the competition. On the other hand, do chart *dry* "brickyards." Since there's no oil to be moved, the lanes will influence your ball the same way all the time. If you can find a way to make the quirks of a brickyard work to your advantage, you're in business.

It is necessary to experiment with the release to find out how to deal with extremely oily conditions. It might be a good idea to check with your favorite house and find out when the lanes are going to be freshly oiled. Then practice on them at that time. Since most novice bowlers do not have strong releases, and have trouble with changing speeds, oil will give them the most trouble. Get all the practice you can on this type of condition; it is far better than waiting until league night, when you can't experiment, and having the condition knock sixty to seventy pins off your total score.

BALL SPEED

Speed refers to the time it takes the ball to go from the point of release at the foul line to the headpin. It is *not* how fast you walk to the foul line, although speed is affected by footwork. It is *not* how quickly you go through the act of delivering the ball, although speed is affected by this motion.

The average ball speed of a professional bowler is approximately 2.5 seconds. Some professionals throw a faster ball (2.1), some a slower ball (2.8). The speed can vary almost a full second according to one's style, and still be effective. It isn't really important how fast you throw the ball, but how compatible the speed you select is with respect to the rest of your game: the ball track you throw (three-quarter roller, full roller, spinner), the number of revolutions you throw, how much loft you use, and the characteristics of the ball that you are using (shell, softness, weights, grip), and so on.

One professional, Howard Holmes, consistently throws a three-second ball, which is really slow; but Holmes has skillfully used slow ball speeds for years. So well, in fact, that he has thrown eight sanctioned 300 games! Because of his controlled speed, Holmes was the 1973 California State co-record holder for most 300 games. In contrast to Holmes is another great bowler, Dick Hoover. He can score well throwing speeds of two seconds flat.

Remember: the important consideration isn't just the speed selected, but how that speed fits your style on a particular lane condition.

Speed—As It Affects Ball Pattern / Ball speed is one of the trickiest factors to control in lining up because of its many side effects. When you change ball speed, you change your shot in three ways:

1. The distance the ball skids down the lane changes. Consequently, the amount of roll (and possible hook) it has left at the back end of the lane changes too.

2. The amount of deflection is altered as the ball moves by the headpin and through the stack of pins. Thus the pin action is changed also. For instance, a faster ball deflects more because of a lack of roll and too much skid. This is much like a speeding car attempting to negotiate an icy highway curve during winter: the faster the car goes, the less traction it has.

3. The ball path—the amount of arc the ball exhibits as it rolls down the lane—is dramatically affected. The number of boards crossed will vary with the speed. The slower the ball is thrown, the more boards it will hook (if the ball has spin). The ball will also react to oil distribution on the lanes at different points on its way to the pins.

The trickiest effect of increasing ball speed is on carry power and corner pins. Even top professionals often fail to interpret subtle speed changes and pin action quickly and correctly.

It is hard to change your ball speed without running into trouble. But if you can do it successfully, it is a very effective way to deal with extreme conditions. In general, when the lane is fast because it has too much oil, slow the ball down. When the lane is dry, speed the ball up.

There's an interesting fact about any given lane *and* each bowler's game. Each lane has an upper and lower speed limit! Throw the ball too slow, and the ball "rolls out" (end over end). Throw it too fast and it skids out. So "police" your speed to stay within those limits.

Three Techniques for Changing Speed (Figure 7–2)

1. Height of Pushaway / The most important point to remember when altering ball speed (Figure 7–2 A) is that as you change your armswing, you must also change the speed of your footwork. Otherwise, you'll foul up your timing!

If you start your pushaway from a higher position, this causes your backswing to be higher, and increases your ball speed. Remember to walk a bit slower to accommodate the greater length of time it will take to complete your armswing.

Of course, the lower your pushaway, the faster your footwork must be. This gives you a rough impression of how to change speeds. You must work out the details for yourself to see what holds true for your game.

2. Length of the Approach Line / You can also change the length of your approach (Figure 7–2 B). You could move up to the twelve-foot dots, or so far back that your heels are hanging off the end of the approach. The closer you start your approach to the foul line, the slower the ball speed (all other things being the same).

These first two methods are the most popular for changing speed, even among professionals.

3. Muscling the Ball—on the Downswing / This is the least popular technique for changing speeds (Figure 7–2 C), especially with bowlers who stroke with a smooth style. Bowlers who tend to accelerate their armswing throughout the trigger position naturally can fit this method into their games more easily, but even they must watch out for critical timing problems. Sometimes, excitement alone can cause a bowler to muscle the

Three ways to change ball speeds:

Figure 7–2A
Change the height of the pushaway

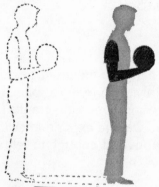

Figure 7–2B
Change the length of your approach

Figure 7–2C
Muscle the ball on the downswing

ball just enough to increase his ball speed. When this happens after you have been stringing strikes, you may lose your carry power and begin leaving corner pins (light 7-pin and a weak 10-pin) on the same pocket hits.

Comment / When beginners attempt to get more ball speed, they often commit four common errors.

> *1. They run, instead of walk, on the approach.*
> *2. They hop in their third step.*
> *3. They open up their right shoulder at the top of the backswing (move it back off line) and then fail to bring it back correctly. Gary Dickinson is a master at opening and closing his shoulder perfectly.)*
> *4. They muscle the ball on the downswing in a jerky motion and lose control. (Experts muscle with a smoother, controlled stroke. Mark Roth is the best at this.)*

STYLE

This is the most difficult change to make successfully. If your natural game is to stroke the ball smoothly, then trying to plant your left foot to get extra leverage on the shot—like someone who cranks the ball—requires totally different timing. You might want to experiment with it in practice, but don't count on being able to "groove" it enough to rely on it in competition.

CHANGING BALLS

Many pros carry extra balls to cope with different conditions. Balls with different grips, different weight distributions, and different shells all have their advantages on varying lane conditions.

If you plan to use only one ball, a moderately soft-shelled ball with zero weight distribution is recommended. If you normally use a fingertip grip, so much the better. A little right thumb-pitch can be useful on some conditions, since this helps to turn the ball.

BALL FACTORS: A CLOSEUP VIEW

Briefly, let us look at how ball factors work on different lane conditions.

Fingertip Grip / This helps on fast conditions because it increases roll and hooking power. A bowler changing from a conventional to a fingertip will be amazed at the difference it creates in the hook. It will not cause problems of any great magnitude on a dry condition, unless the lane is extremely dry. Then the ball will hook sooner and more widely.

Conventional Grip / Easier to control, but doesn't produce as much hooking power. A disadvantage on fast conditions. Some experts will use it to combat very slow conditions, but since this grip calls for a different release than the fingertip, the change is difficult to make without a great deal of practice.

Right Thumb-Pitch / Makes it easier to turn the ball early in the release. If this causes you to overturn the ball, making it skid too far, adjusting to oily conditions may become more difficult.

Zero or Left-Thumb Pitch / Causes your hand to stay behind the ball longer, thus reducing turn and giving the ball greater forward roll. This will help on slow conditions by killing the hook. Some professionals say that it helps on both fast and slow conditions, but the effect is minor when compared with the other factors. This kind of pitch is notorious for tearing up thumbs.

Positive Side or Finger Weight / Extends the skid, but also makes the ball hook sharply on the back end. This is desirable on slow conditions if it doesn't create too much hook. On fast conditions it may cause the ball to skid much too far—creating a "sixty-five-foot skid-line on a sixty-foot alley." Some leading bowlers like a zero-weighted ball on a fast condition. Others, wanting to get the extra hooking power this weight provides, will use it on a fast condition, but only if they can get it into a roll, which is difficult for some.

Negative Side or Thumb Weight / Shortens the skid, gets the ball into an earlier roll, but detracts from hooking power and deflects more at the back end. Has both advantages and disadvantages on both types of conditions. Experiment to see which works best for you. (It is interesting to note that most pros who have experimented with weights have either gone back to zero or positive weights. Part of this is due to all the problems created by extreme conditions.)

Ball Hardness / Shell hardness will affect how soon the ball begins to roll and the degree of deflection at the pins. The softer the shell, the sooner it will roll, and the more it will hook and drive. A harder-shelled ball will skid farther and deflect more.

THE STRATEGY IN BRICKYARDS AND BLOCKS

There are two extreme lane-conditions that call for special strategies—brickyards and blocked lanes.

Brickyards / There is almost no way to play brickyards logically. Open-grain boards, spotty oil, and dry spots create such extreme variations in ball action that you can rarely get lined up.

If your opening line on a brickyard is obviously not going to work, then change it. You have nothing to lose. You may find a line that gets you to the pocket, but with minimal carry. Now, the situation becomes tricky. Do you stay with that line, grinding out mediocre scores in the hope that your scores will better all other scores, or do you fish for a new angle?

There is danger in both alternatives. If you go fishing, you can easily end up bowling 40 pins below your average. Every time you try something new that doesn't work, it loses another strike and maybe another mark. This may cause you to become too careful. If you stay with your original line and lose out, you'll kick yourself for not having had the courage to move. It's a tough choice, but if you fish for a new line, do it confidently and intelligently. Maybe you'll see something in another bowler's shot that will give you a clue. If so, try it. But groping blindly for a line on a brickyard is almost always disastrous.

Blocked Lanes / When you're on blocked lanes where players are shooting "telephone numbers" (250's and up), the strategy is simple. Don't settle for any line other than the edge of the oil wall. That's the only line. What would normally be a good score (220) becomes a loser's score on blocked lanes. So your only strategy on blocked lanes is to find the wall and stay with it.

Walls will dry up. In doing so, the edge usually retreats to the left. I have played on walls where, for the morning squad, the line was the 10-board. By the evening, the scoring was taking place on the edge of the wall at the 18-board. This means the wall dried up 8 boards to the left. It was gradual, so my adjustments had to be gradual also.

8. ADVANCED CONCEPTS

It sounds obvious, but a good bowler always has something that his less successful opponents lack. Yes, there are differences in sheer physical ability, but that's not the main point. After all, just about everyone has met a bowler who is loaded with natural ability but is still unable to put it all together.

The fact is that to reach his full potential every bowler must have a complete understanding of the game. He has to know as much as he can about the pins, the lanes, the type of release he uses, and so on. Otherwise, like a doctor faced with a strange disease, he won't know what action to take when things go wrong.

Of course no one can ever achieve a complete understanding of the game. The subject is just too complex, and total understanding may not really be necessary. But a good bowler is constantly trying to increase his knowledge. He is continually observing and experimenting with what he's learned.

It's this lifelong quest for a clearer understanding of the game that separates low-average bowlers from the trophy winners and the pros. This is where all "professional secrets" come from, for, as in any other field, the tricks of the trade are really nothing more than an exceptionally wide knowledge of the subject.

What follows are some of the things I've learned during my career. Reading them might be a help. But to make these trade secrets really work, I strongly suggest practicing them thoroughly. You may not get everything right the first few times you try one of these techniques, but eventually you'll discover that they can work wonders for your game.

WHAT HAPPENED TO MY STRIKES?

It happens to everyone—pros and amateurs alike. You're lined up perfectly. Your stroke is smooth and your carry power at the pocket is tremendous. Then—all of a sudden—no more strikes!

Now in place of those beautiful pocket strikes, you're getting a light 7-pin leave, a packed 10-pin spare, and a stubborn 4-pin. What happened?

Well, probably a number of things: a chain reaction of errors.

First, you've started to put together an impressive string of strikes, and you're eager to keep it going. So in your excitement you begin to rush a bit.

You unconsciously start to speed up the first two steps in your approach. This puts your footwork ahead of your armswing. And, since your body arrives at the foul line a little before your arm, you begin to pull the ball just ever so slightly harder and sooner in the downswing.

You're now forcing your armswing and not finishing the shot with the same subtle lift action you had been using so successfully earlier in the game—a lift action that produced better roll on the ball as it entered the pocket.

All of which keeps you from getting the necessary leverage on the ball as you slide. Thus you're not able to get under and behind the ball properly in the trigger position.

When your ball speed increases slightly, this results in a little more skid and a little less hook and roll on the back end. And you're probably throwing the ball with one or two fewer revolutions by being too careful— "fitting the shot," as it's called.

These errors in your physical game are so slight and so difficult to detect that it takes a real expert to notice what's happening. Yet the results of these errors can devastate your score and, perhaps worst of all, leave you bewildered about what you're doing wrong.

The thing to remember is a phrase as old as bowling itself: "Take one shot at a time." When it's your turn to throw, clear your mind of everything that has come before and anything you hope will come after. Only then will you avoid this subtle chain reaction that causes so many bowlers to lose their carry power and break their string and concentration.

BALL PATTERNS

The shape of the ball pattern (Figure 8–1) as it rolls down the lane is one of the least understood and least discussed concepts in bowling. Yet, it is one of the most important things to know. The ball describes a path on the lane. It can be a straight path, or it may be straight two thirds of the way and curve as it covers the last third.

Often it is difficult to know when you are creating the wrong ball pattern for the condition. You may be hitting the pocket well, but have trouble carrying strikes. I remember a tournament in which all the top scores were coming off the second arrow for right-handers; one touring pro kept murdering the pocket at that angle. Yet, all he could get was a 10-pin, or a 4-pin leave, and only an occasional strike. He had absolutely no carry power from that angle. He went in to the third-arrow—it got worse. Then he went out to the first arrow—still no improvement. Eventually, he went back to the second arrow and waited for the tournament to end.

The trouble, in my opinion, was that all the finalists were hooking the ball on the back end (near the pins). This fellow was trying to score with a line ball. For that particular condition, a line ball was just not the shot. Of couse, there have been situations in which the opposite was true. That is, the line ball carried much better than the big hooker. Fortunately, most house conditions permit either shot to score if you are bowling well.

Don't think of the following as hard and fast rules, but rather as a series of guidelines. Illustration 8–1 shows the four basic ball patterns.

1. The Fallback Shot—Fourth Arrow / This ball pattern is played usually near the fourth arrow. The ball crosses the boards from left to right on the front part of the lane, then in the last twenty feet it rolls parallel with the boards to the pocket. This deep inside shot sets up (stops

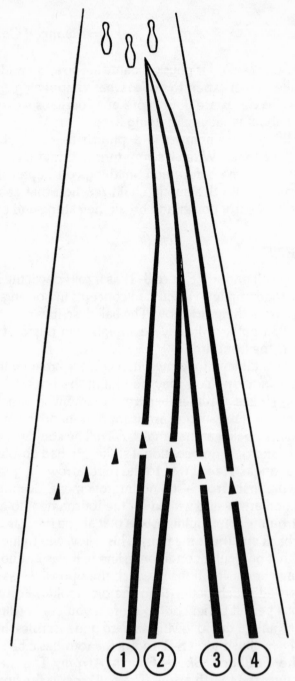

Figure 8–1   Ball patterns

hooking left) farther out, and holds that line all the way to the pocket. For this reason it is sometimes called a "fallback" shot.

An interesting variation of the fallback shot occurred in a tournament in Buffalo, New York. This ball pattern was used by most of the finalists between the fourth arrow and LEFT of the fifth arrow. If that shot wasn't unusual enough, Nelson Burton, Jr., chose to walk a zigzag approach around and to the left of the ball return on the right lane, in order to get deep enough with his angle. Ever try to make the finals doing that all night? Burton did!

2. *The Swing Shot—Third Arrow* / This ball may be thrown anywhere from the second arrow to the fifth arrow, depending on the condition. The ball crosses the boards from left to right, then, after it gets down the lane some distance, it begins crossing the boards right to left. Here it hooks sharply on its way back to the headpin. Some bowlers are able to change the shape of this shot so that it doesn't loop out as much. That is, the arc is straightened so that it has less curvature than shown in the illustration. When this is done, then you may see the swing shot played effectively from the first arrow all the way in to the fifth arrow. This is the only shot pro bowlers seem to change radically and still score well.

3. *The Line Ball—Second Arrow* / This ball pattern is very effective around the second arrow. The ball rolls parallel to the boards for the first two thirds of the lane and then hooks to the pocket. Depending on the amount of oil, this shot can be played so that your target is to the right or left of the second arrow. That is, you could be pointing the ball up the 7-board or straight up the 12-board. It is a rare bowler who can change a natural line-ball to bellying the ball.

4. *The Point Shot—First Arrow* / This pattern is played only on outside lines near the first arrow. It is the shot used when a bowler points the ball up to the pocket. It may have very little hook or it may have as much as shown in the illustration. There is no belly, or arcing the ball—otherwise, the ball ends up in the gutter on errant shots that have missed the target to the right. Gary Dickinson is one of the best at letting the ball hang over the right edge of the lane and then hook the back end big. However, I bowled in Denver one year and watched Nelson Burton, Jr., incredibly play a line for six games, in which he successfully lofted the ball over the right gutter onto the 1- and 2-board!!! Not only is that gutty, that's talent. Needless to say, in the fourth game on six in a row, he put one in the sewer, but came right back to strike and not alter his angle one bit.

It is interesting to note that there are many bowlers who can throw only one of the four basic ball patterns. These are the same bowlers who have trouble maintaining their scoring ability from outside the first arrow to inside the fourth arrow. In fact, most bowlers who have stopped studying the game become either exclusively inside shooters or strictly outside shooters.

RELEASES AND BALL TRACKS

The circular track that you may observe on your ball comes from the ball contacting the lane as it rolls toward the pins. The track can give you a clue as to the type of release you're throwing. And as most experienced bowlers know, this is highly significant in analyzing their game.

How to Change from a Full Roller to a Three-Quarter Roller / Since most professional bowlers throw a three-quarter roller, you are probably interested in trying to throw one yourself. If you now throw a full roller, this change can be made with practice, once you understand the difference in the release.

The Full Roller Release / Imagine a clock face on your ball. To get into the full-roller release position, you would break your wrist slightly, with your hand hanging down at your side. The thumb should be between the nine- and eleven-o'clock position, and your fingers between the three- and five-o'clock position. This position is held throughout the pushaway, backswing, and much of the downswing. The thumb remains in the ball until relatively late in the release. The fingers rotate under the thumb in a clockwise direction—but no farther than six o'clock, or you will throw a back-up ball. The ball will have nearly complete forward roll, with the ball track (Figure 8–2) appearing to the left of the finger holes, and to the right of the thumb hole.

The Three-Quarter Roller Release / To throw a three-quarter roller, the bowler positions his hand in the ball so that the thumb lies between eleven and twelve o'clock, and the fingers between five and six o'clock. The ball is held in this manner from the pushaway until the bottom of the downswing. At this point, the thumb is released. Then, with just the

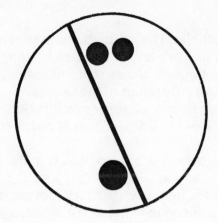

Figure 8–2   The full-roller ball track

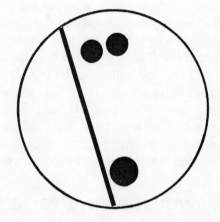

Figure 8–3   The three-quarter-roller ball track

fingers in the ball, the bowler turns his wrist counter clockwise so that his palm is facing left and his thumb is pointing upward. This is often referred to as the "handshake" position, where the bowler pretends to be shaking hands with someone out on the lane.

While the wrist is turning late in the release, the fingers quickly apply added lift to the ball—smoothly, without jerking. Jerking can cause the ball to be pulled off line. The thumb clears the release much earlier in a three-quarter roller than in a full roller.

In the three-quarter roller, the ball is spinning as the finger holes are moving ahead of the thumb hole. This causes it to roll in a sideways fashion down the lane (Figure 8–3). Thus, a track develops on the left, or outside, of both the thumb and finger holes. The key to the success of both types of shots lies, however, in the bowler's ability to extend during his follow-through. An extended follow-through allows more time for your hand to stay in the ball during the most critical part of the release.

This much of the conversion from a full roller to a three-quarter roller is easy enough. But there is one final aspect that is much more difficult: timing.

If you've been throwing a full roller all your bowling life, you naturally have full-roller timing. That is, you stroke during your slide. In order to throw a three-quarter roller, you must plant your left foot earlier at the line in order to establish leverage during the release. That means your stroke will come a little later in the slide.

Some pros who have attempted the conversion have found that they were able to produce the three-quarter-roller track but that their ball was too weak. They weren't getting their left foot planted early enough, so they weren't able to get enough leverage on the ball.

You can successfully vary your ball speed. But you can't change your timing without a lot of practice. So, if you're going to try converting a full roller to a three-quarter roller, you should work on it during the off season. That way, you won't foul yourself up for a league night. Changing your timing and release successfully is possible for only a very few talented bowlers. It isn't recommended.

"HIGHLIGHTING" THE POCKET

When the ball looks fine as it covers the first half of the lane but suddenly jumps left or hangs out to the right as it approaches the pins, the ball is "highlighting" the pocket (Figure 8–4). The problem is difficult to understand, but it is the best indication for you to alter your line. Otherwise, the tolerance for error will be low. This means that when you miss your target just a little, the ball misses the pocket by a lot. Slight variations in ball speeds produce an overreaction when you are playing the wrong part of the lane.

There are two factors responsible for a shot going wrong. Either your execution was bad, or you were playing the wrong angle. Learning to separate results due to bad execution from results caused by playing the wrong angle is essential to reading lanes.

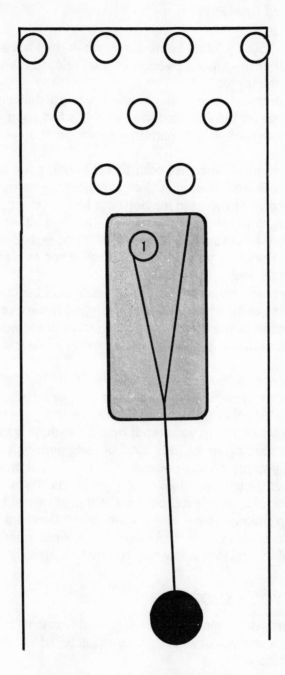

Figure 8–4   Highlighting the pocket

Most bowlers know immediately when they have thrown the ball incorrectly: Either they feel it as soon as they release the ball, or they see their ball miss the target.

When you feel you have made a good delivery and are sure you've hit the target but find that the ball grabs too soon or too late (and not on just one shot, but a pattern), conclude that you are lined up incorrectly.

For example, suppose your ball is hooking too much and going through the nose and Brooklyn. Yet every time you try to correct this problem (before you have tried moving your feet or target), your correction shot hangs out to the right of the pocket—leaving either the bucket, the fence, or the washout (bucket = 2–4–5–8; fence = 1–2–4–7; washout = 1–2–4–10). It seems to you that every small error made at the foul line becomes exaggerated at the pocket.

This is when the ball-to-floor relationship becomes very critical. Missing your target by a half board, or changing the speed slightly, results in an overreaction of the ball as it moves in front of the pocket. When that happens, assume that you've selected the wrong angle and begin adjusting your line.

Sometimes you can prevent the ball from highlighting the pocket by adjusting your back position a board or two, or by adjusting your hand position a little. At other times, it requires a major adjustment at the target (changing arrows or where you stand) or even switching to another ball.

Like reading lanes, this kind of judgment will only come with experience. If you are an inexperienced bowler, you'll probably fault your execution when you have highlighting problems. As a result you'll become overly careful, which will only make things worse. Highlighting is a fairly common phenomenon, and it more often than not indicates a bad line, not bad execution. This is obviously true, since only a few thousand bowlers out of the millions know how to line up correctly.

CHECKING YOUR SHOT

How do the pros determine exactly what went wrong with a shot? They go through a quick analysis of what they saw their ball do and what they felt at the point of release.

The emphasis placed on each factor differs with every expert bowler. Even the order in which he thinks of them differs. Therefore, the following is only a list of what to analyze. These items are not necessarily given in the order that you should think of them. But each of them deserves attention.

Just after releasing the ball check:

●*Speed—See if you got the desired ball speed.*

●*Timing—Did the timing of your armswing and footwork feel coordinated?*

●*Mark—Watch the ball as it rolls over the target to see if it was missed.*

●*Release—Did you cut the release off too soon, set it short, pull it, top it, etc.?*

●*Approach line—Did you drift away from or into your intended approach line?*

If you're satisfied with these factors and the shot still went wrong, then the problem must be the lane condition and thus the angle you were playing.

HINTS ON SPARE SHOOTING

Many professionals shoot all corner-pin spares cross alley. Most books cover this subject adequately. But the pictures and illustrations they provide ignore the factor of lane condition. They present spare-shooting as though it were taking place in a vacuum.

There are, in fact, three difficult conditions you must adjust for:

1. *Very dry lanes.* Since the ball will hook more than usual, any of the following will be necessary: more speed, more forward roll, kill your shot, increase loft but not lift, throw the ball more to the right to allow for the hooking condition (this works when the lanes are not spotty). Be careful that you don't use too little ball speed; otherwise the night will be spent missing spares to the left of the spare pin.

2. *Very oily lanes.* It is always easier to make spares on an evenly oiled condition, after you've tightened up your back position (moved right with your feet while keeping your target in the same place). You don't have

to make any other allowances for the shot. You simply throw the ball straight at the pin. Also, the effects of speed errors are minimized. On oil most shots tend to act alike whether they have spin or forward roll—they all skid and go straight at the pin. If you can hook a ball on oil, you are a rarity.

3. *Blocked lanes.* This is the trickiest condition to shoot spares on, especially when you are attempting to convert left-side spares like the 7-pin, 4–7, and 2–4–5.

Remember, dry conditions will cause the ball to hook too much. Therefore, when you miss a spare on dry conditions, you usually miss it to the left.

On a blocked condition, the exact opposite is true. The ball never seems to hook enough. In fact, sometimes the ball appears to back up. I have played on "walls" that were so heavily oiled that I had to aim the ball uncomfortably to the left of my target, especially when shooting the 7-pin. On a normal condition, the ball would most certainly go into the gutter. But on this condition, there is almost no hook, so it stays on the lane and picks up the spare.

One of the first tip-offs that you are contending with a "wall" comes when you throw your first cross-alley spare shot. On an evenly oiled condition, you know from your strike ball that oil is present. But when the lane is blocked, you may not discover it until your first cross-alley shot. The result startles you, because you expected the ball to hook, but it just "falls back" as it encounters the oil and misses by a foot to the right.

AREA

"Area" is a term used to describe the successful effects of proper lineup. It is used to describe both your floor target and your headpin target. Not everybody uses the same floor target, but everybody aims for the same general pocket. It is easy to get these two concepts—"area on the floor" and "area at the pocket"—mixed up. Because of this, it might be wise to clarify briefly the difference between the two.

Area at the Pocket / Having area at the pocket means that the percentage of carry on all three parts of the pocket is good. The high-, middle-, and light-pocket zones are all producing strikes. You can carry a packed shot from any angle, but lose your percentage of carry on high and light hits when you are not "lined up." Players differ as to what part of the pocket they play for, but they all want "area at the pocket" if they can get it. For instance, a bowler who uses a straighter ball pattern might play his shot for a deep middle-pocket shot and high wall shots (4-pin trip and 4-7 strikes). A bowler with a bigger hook might play a tiny bit farther to the right of that, setting up his impact point in the middle pocket for "late tens" and half-pocket wall shots (5–7), rippers (throwing the 5-pin at the 7-pin), and light hits (swishing 7-pins).

　　　An easy way to keep these terms clear is to think of area on the floor as either "pull area" or "swing area," while "area at the pocket" is just simply that.

　　　Area on the Floor / This (Figure 8–5) refers to your target on the lane when you have lined up properly. It is totally dependent on the lane

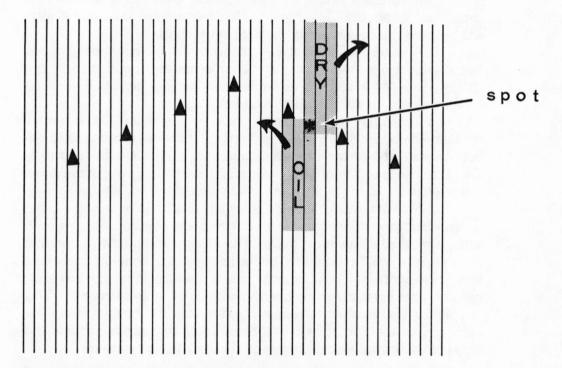

spot

Figure 8–5   The "area on the floor" varies with the condition. You can miss a board or two left on oil and hit the pocket for a strike. You can miss a board or two right on dry conditions and hit the pocket for a strike

condition. On a normal lane condition, creating area on the floor means you can miss your target a board to the left or to the right of where you aimed and still get back to some portion of the pocket and carry for a strike. On an oil condition the "pull area" on the floor is only to the left of your target line; and on dry lanes the "swing area" is only to the right of your target line.

In other words, you can pull a shot a little inside your line on oil and the ball won't overreact ("run Brooklyn") as it would on dry. But if you miss a board to the right—goodbye. Conversely, you can swing the ball away from the pocket on dry lanes and it will still get back and carry strikes. But if you set your shot a board inside your line, it runs over on the nose or Brooklyn every time. Having area is when you can miss your target and still hold the pocket.

If the entire lane is slick, then the ball pattern will be somewhat straighter for both the hooker and the line-ball shooter; thus both players will be setting up their shots for middle-pocket shots.

Area on the floor is an advantageous thing to have going for you because it catches most of your execution errors and converts them into strikes. However, it remains dependent on the lane condition—and on how it matches up with your particular ball.

The following is a simple rule to remember: On a normal medium-oiled condition, a one-board error at the target produces a three-board error at the pocket. However, on a condition that is either unusually dry in the heads or is termed a "brickyard," a one-board error at the target will result in a five- to six-board error to the left of the pocket.

Knowing what influence "creating area" has on scoring, it becomes obvious why 300 games are shot, and why bowlers' averages soar, when a blocked condition is put in. The heavy concentration of oil that makes up the "wall" creates area on the left, while the bone-dry part of the lane to the right of the "wall" creates area to the right. When this happens, players have been observed bowling with a 4- or 5-board area! This establishes "pull area" on the left and "swing area" on the right. It can't be made any easier to score than this. Since accuracy is now automatic, the only possible errors are caused by speed variations and anxieties.

HOW TO RATE A BOWLER

In any PBA tournament, you can rate a professional bowler's chances of winning by considering four key factors: lane conditions, current form, class, and range.

Lane Conditions / Nobody has ever identified and named every possible lane condition that currently exists throughout the nation, let alone told you how to play each type correctly. Lane conditions can make or break a bowler, and there isn't a bowler in the world who can completely overcome this factor. This means that only a few outstanding bowlers have the versatility to maintain high scoring averages on many different conditions. Therefore, when trying to rate a bowler, consider whether his game fits the condition. If not, then how quickly can he adjust his game to score well?

Pins must be included in this category because of the intimate relationship between lane conditions and the effect of pin weight on a bowler's ability to score. A lighter pin flies higher up from the floor and mixes worse for bowlers who throw a strong ball, especially on dry lanes.

Current Form / Like race horses, you can expect pro bowlers to perform according to their "current form." If a bowler is in a hot streak you can usually expect him to finish high in the standings. On the other hand, even the best bowlers fall into slumps and bowl badly. This might be due to a flaw in their physical execution or to simple psychological factors. Practice alone is often not sufficient to pull a bowler out of a slump. The bowler may have to consult with a teacher who knows his game. Or he may have to deal with psychological factors to the best of his ability, or take a rest.

Class / Class is a very real factor in a bowler's performance. It is a combination of experience, confidence, self-image, respect of peers, career average, total winnings, and number of titles won. Many times class is the factor that decides the outcome of a tournament, especially when several bowlers are "hitting the condition" equally well.

Since pros must always perform under competitive pressure, this is where class shows. It actually creates a pecking order among bowlers, just as in all competitive activities. When everything else is equal, the higher-class bowler will almost always beat the lower-class bowler. Regardless of how well a bowler may have scored on a given pair of lanes, when a lower-class bowler needs a strike to beat a higher-class bowler, he usually can't get it. And even when the winning score is low (below 200), the higher-class bowler usually comes out on top. The same holds true for all bowlers, whether amateur or pro.

Range / Range is the ability of a bowler to score on many different conditions—oily or dry, blocked or unblocked, tracked or resurfaced. Range is the ability to change ball speed, use different hand positions and releases, different ball patterns, and different types of weights in the ball.

The more range a bowler can develop without destroying his natural game, the better off he will be.

PROFESSIONAL POINTERS . . . ON TECHNIQUE

●When experimenting, new methods may feels strange to you. This is the greatest obstacle to improvement.

●Rush to get to the lanes, and you've set the wrong tempo for the night!

●Always play to win. You're remembered for your achievements, not your failures.

●Push yourself physically to get through the shot each time.

●A change in lane condition measures a bowler's range and knowledge . . . and his patience.

●Bad execution is often blamed for a poor performance, when in reality it was due to a failure to line up properly.

●Every type of delivery has its strengths and its weaknesses, and only under pressure do you realize what they are.

●Orthodox form has been developed over generations. Think before you decide that you're the exception to the rule.

●Don't gripe. Think of a solution and apply it to your game.

●"Feel" isn't produced in a day.

●It's unbelievable how long people will tolerate a bad feel in their grip, thinking "It's just me," when it's really due to improper drilling.

●In the execution phase of a physical sport, there is only one time frame: the here and now.

●Good game management is knowing your limitations and playing within your strengths.

●Everybody puts his fingers into the ball . . . but only a few put their fingers into the shot. Don't forget to extend before you lift.

●Don't beat yourself. There will be plenty of people already trying to do that.

9. THE MENTAL GAME— PART 1

You often hear an athlete say "Ninety percent of my game is mental." After the game the winner often talks more about how he handled himself psychologically than about his physical performance. He'll talk about his strategy, how he kept his cool when things went wrong, how he coped with pressure, or how he kept it going once he got it going.

On the other hand, many great athletes fall into slumps. A few never recover. Even stars occasionally "choke" under the intense pressures of competition. How many times have you seen an entire professional basketball team suddenly tighten up and draw iron on their shots, even when they have been ahead the entire game? This may be due to faulty strategy, or superior strategy or play by the opposition, but often it is purely psychological—the effect of pressure.

To be successful in any competitive sport, you must master yourself. And the greater your skill becomes the more crucial your mental game is, particularly as you engage in higher and higher levels of competition. It is one thing to bowl for a reputation as an amateur. It is quite another to bowl professionally, with thousands of dollars and your livelihood on the line, and to be able to cope psychologically with that kind of pressure—tournament after tournament, year after year. However, even the office league amateur senses and reacts to the pressure of a challenge to his ego before his peer group, and the mental game is a big factor in his success or failure, too.

This chapter explains the thought control used in winning performances. The ideas presented here are simple facts about the way the mind works in certain types of games. They do not cover a fast-reaction type of sport like boxing; we are concerned here with the mental game of bowling, and games that are similar.

In bowling, as in golf, you don't compete directly against an opponent; you face nonhuman obstacles like tricky lane conditions, or a doglegged fairway, or a sloping green, or light pins. Add to that the fact that you spend most of your time sitting on the bench and watching, or walking down the fairway—times when internal pressures can build—and you have games in which competitiveness must be combined with self-control. In contact sports you can relieve pressure by exploding at an opponent. In bowling and golf your only physical outlet is throwing a sixteen-pound ball or swinging a golf club, both with great precision.

Uncontrolled competitiveness interferes, not helps, in these sports. If you let yourself get carried away, you can begin rushing your shot, pulling it off target, or forgetting fine points in your delivery that you have made to cope with lane conditions.

When Arnold Palmer was at the peak of his career he thrived on competitiveness. He needed his famous "charge" when coming from behind against unbelievable odds, and creating high tension and excitement in the gallery, which became known as "Arnie's Army." His greatest asset was "slam-dunking" tricky downhill putts. And if he missed and went by the cup six feet, he'd "slam-dunk" it coming back. No one in the history of golf could "will" the ball into the hole the way Palmer could. A "lag-putt" wasn't part of his vocabulary.

Palmer, of course, is no longer ranked at the top. Who really knows why? No one can continually bang the ball into the back of the cup and not have it wear on his nerves. Watching Palmer on the green today, you sense that the ball isn't going in the cup and you also sense that Palmer knows it, too. Many golf theorists claim that professionals burn themselves out. Each professional golfer has an emotional life span, and when it goes, so does his putting skill. From tee to green, he can be as good as ever, but it is on the greens with the sensitive, delicate, intensity-building putts that burned-out nerves really show themselves.

In bowling, a champion can sometimes lose his stroke while stringing strikes. Now strikes are interrupted by corner pins for spares (4-, 7-, or 10-pin). This means one thing: burned-out nerves.

COPING WITH PRESSURE

All athletes feel the effects of pressure to some extent. In fact, you should worry if you didn't feel pressure, because this might indicate lack of motivation to win. On the day of an important match, you may feel absolutely terrible. Nausea and tiredness are common. Some athletes actually vomit before a contest. Others may feel slightly jumpy and restless. All of which simply indicates that your body is preparing itself for the contest. Once the contest starts, these feelings should subside.

In sports like bowling and golf, the body may overreact to mounting pressure. Since you spend most of your time sitting or walking in these sports, with plenty of time to think, a high adrenaline level and an overactive imagination can work against you. You can lose control and not execute properly. Many athletes, through trial and error, have developed ways of coping with this problem, with varying degrees of success.

To hold off pressure, and the damage it can do to your game, keep several things in mind.

Concentrate on the Here and Now / Whether things are going well or poorly for you, it can be devastating to think about either the past or the future. Here are two examples of mental errors which will inevitably kill a string of strikes:

1. "If I can just keep this up, I'll get my first 300 game!" Avoid this line of thought. Think about this frame alone or, if you're sitting down, try to keep your mind as calm and still as possible.

2. "The reason this is happening is that new release I've developed. Turning my wrist more and getting more leverage . . ." Analyzing like that can be just as bad, because your body, timing, release, line, and

everything else are grooved. Trying to analyze why you are stroking well can break that groove. It is traditional in baseball not to talk to a pitcher who has a perfect game going. He is in a nonverbal state of mind, and he wants to stay there. Trying to make him think about the hoped-for outcome creates needless tension and can break his concentration. He wants to concentrate fully on one pitch at a time.

If things aren't going well for you, resist drawing negative, depressing conclusions. There is either something wrong in your physical execution, which is correctable, or you haven't found the line, which you can calmly make plans for finding—changing your floor position, altering your speed slightly, or whatever else is called for. But be cautious about big alterations. When the wheels begin to loosen, they can fall off entirely if you emotionally and physically try to make huge changes in your style or playing pattern.

This is not the time to start brooding, criticizing yourself, and thinking about how poor your eventual score is going to be. Such thinking snowballs and practically insures a bad score. All you can do is to think constructively about how you're going to make your next shot a success.

Some Zen Concepts / Zen thinking emphasizes the importance of singleness of thought. And this has direct application to stilling your mind so as not to trigger wild emotional thoughts. The Zen notion of "the here and now" calls for viewing things in their present time frame only.

Athletes who view athletic events sequentially often get into trouble mentally. Instead of concentrating exclusively on the immediate task before them (getting a strike in this frame, or making this putt), they often will link a series of disconnected events both in the past and in the imaginary future. These thoughts have absolutely no relevance to the present situation.

For instance, a bowler might try to figure out if he is having a bad day by listing every possible mental mistake both on and off the lanes. It is possible to build any kind of case for yourself, good or bad. An undisciplined mind often fluctuates at the slightest turn of events, with little staying power or tenacity.

Another Zen concept designed to eliminate entire lines of detrimental thought is the notion of "it." "It" released the arrow. "It" made the putt. "It" flung the spear. "It" threw the ball. This strange wording seems closely related to the mental ploy that many American athletes use. Only you hear it expressed in this form: "My putter just wasn't working for me today." "I had the wrong ball on those lanes." "That bat just didn't feel comfortable in my hands." In other words, the player was OK, it was his equipment that was acting up!

This ability to remain aloof and blame it on the things external to oneself often works. As patently deceptive as it is, it still seems to succeed for the player who believes what he is saying, at least temporarily.

However, to be precise, the Zen notion of "it" is directly concerned with the elimination of ego or the "Big I." This means there is no elation with success nor depression with failure. You maintain an even emotional posture of detached confidence. Athletes who have trained their minds to be undisturbed by the emotional overtones of a contest are free to execute to the best of their physical ability.

This philosophy is suited to those who perform better by emotionally detaching themselves from the scene of battle. Such people execute in accordance with what they believe to be the perfect shot, regardless of its consequences. For those who have had difficulty with the emotional side effects of pressure, this is a valid method of coping. It is, however, an indirect, defensive approach to winning. This is not to say that it is bad. But there is another equally effective mental attitude for maximizing one's performance.

Taking the Offensive / This attitude is characterized by going "heads up," match play, getting pumped up, getting the juices flowing, gutting it out, being overly courageous, gambling confidently, seeing who has more class, or who will crack first. This is an aggressive, winning attitude, and it is just as valid as detachment.

There is a limitation, though: You don't always execute well enough to support this approach. During those times of less than perfect execution you will suffer the consequences of having overextended your skills. Also, you can get overpumped to the extent that your relaxed, smooth execution becomes unpredictable or muscled. There are times when a performer must win by playing well within himself. No player can expect to produce his best shot on every occasion. It depends on how sharp you are currently.

The drawback in Zen detachment is that you may not be able to rise to the occasion by tapping those instinctive emotional reservoirs where you outdo yourself. The same person may use both methods alternately; you can win with either. It is just a question of which fits your personality and the situation that confronts you.

PROFESSIONAL POINTERS ON HANDLING PRESSURE

● Pressure results from imagination on the loose, and from anticipation of failure instead of success.

● When you let tension build with each strike, you become ego-bound, thought-bound, and bound to crack.

● Count the number of thoughts you have under pressure. The fewer the number, the less you're feeling the pressure. Then stop counting.

● Don't put yourself under pressure during competition. There will be many situations that will produce it without your help.

● Mentally "betting the farm" guarantees pressure. Opportunities come over and over again, so relax.

KEEPING A CHANNELED MIND

You may not think "words" to yourself as you prepare to bowl. You may just "visualize" the floor adjustment, "feel" your shot internally, and "picture" how it's going to look.

Whatever you do, don't start visualizing how to miss. If you've been observing lane conditions, you should be certain of how to shoot a 10-pin spare—what spot to hit, where to stand, and so on. But if you worry about how you might miss it, you're increasing your chances of doing just that. You'll pull the shot, rush the line, or make some other error. But you won't make the 10-pin. Usually, what you imagine determines what you do.

There is a story about Jack Nicklaus that illustrates this point. While playing in the 1975 Ryder Cup matches, he was left with a twenty-foot putt. A friend needled him with a comment like "You've missed those before, haven't you, Jack?" He looked up at his antagonist and answered: "I've never missed one in my mind!"

Between frames, it is best not to think, unless you can think calmly and constructively. Even then, it's often better to hold your thinking to a minimum. If you start the internal, verbal dialogue, you may begin disruptive analysis.

In highly competitive leagues, there is a great deal of mutually supportive exchange between team members. Good shots are rewarded with cheers and congratulations. While the sense of competition is keen, there is an attempt to keep the atmosphere light and friendly among team members.

You would think this would break a bowler's concentration, but in reality, it does the opposite. It discourages too much thinking between frames. It keeps all the bowlers loose, so that they are able to think positively. It prevents bowlers from "stewing in their own juices."

When you get into tournament match play, however, it doesn't work that way. Most professionals find this kind of activity distracting, and all are self-reliant enough to maintain a relaxed frame of mind on their own. Many do this by "turning off" their minds between frames, especially when they are lined up. If they are not lined up, their mental activity focuses on what adjustments they should be making, but this thinking is as constructive and anxiety-free as possible.

Whatever you do, you should reject all anxious thought, and limit your thinking to that which is going to help you.

THINKING THE RIGHT THOUGHTS AT THE RIGHT TIME

Mental Cycles / Every sport that requires the athlete to perform a specific maneuver has a common mental set (excluding the "reaction" sports). This set is composed of five sequential events that are repeated in cycles. It doesn't matter whether you are attempting to shoot a free throw, pitch a baseball, stroke a putt, or bowl a strike. The mental set follows the same sequence in each of these sports, and it is the same for every player.

1. "Waiting in the wings." Just as an actor waits in the wings for his cue to go on stage, so is there a mental waiting period for the athlete before he executes his next shot. This period may last from a few seconds to five minutes, depending on the sport. In bowling, you sit and wait for the other player to finish his frame. In golf, you stand and wait for other players to tee off, hit a fairway shot, or putt. This is the time when many athletes damage their performance because they worry about the outcome, how they will look, what people will think, and so on.

It is crucial to remain mentally relaxed during this period. Don't allow counterproductive thoughts to enter your mind.

2. "On your mark, get set . . ." This is the phase that precedes the actual shot-making. It may last only a few seconds or a minute, depending on the sport. In bowling, the player is standing on the approach, ball in hand, making physical and mental preparations for shot execution. This phase of the mental set may begin with some analysis, but by the time you subvocally tell yourself "Go!" the analysis should have stopped and the "feel" should have started. The biggest stumbling block during this phase is thinking about what was wrong with the last shot, rather than concentrating on the upcoming shot.

3. "Shot-making." This is the moment of truth, the time when all your mental preparations come to physical fruition. It is at this point that you *join your mental picture of the shot with the corresponding feel*. There can be no inner dialog at this time; it must be pure "feel," based upon physical certainty.

Even then, once the shot is made, you are still in a game of percentages. There is no certainty that you are going to get a strike, even if you've found the line and are grooved. One of the stumbling blocks at this point is trying for overcontrol. You will hear bowlers say, "You've got to trust yourself. Don't 'fit' the shot. Trust your armswing."

Trying to overcontrol indicates a lack of confidence in the "feel" you have developed, a lack of inner physical certainty, which is crucial at this point. Trying to overcontrol often results in a physical mistake. It's the quickest way to break a string of strikes.

If it's difficult to visualize this concept, think of a golfer who is about to make a forty-foot putt. He sees that he is faced with a long, downhill, curving putt on a fast green. He can pace it off and determine that it is a forty-foot putt. He can survey it from all angles and determine that it will break left three feet. He can note that the green is fast. But he's still not ready to putt.

Why? Because all this analysis serves only as preliminary information which will prepare him to think, "How hard do I hit a putt in order to make it go forty feet, downhill, on a fast green? What does it feel like? Next he will take a few practice strokes to recollect, approximately, the "feel," which is a physical product of his past putting experiences. Now he looks at the hole and traces a line back to the ball. He looks back and forth, from ball to hole, over and over, until he "pictures" the roll of the ball, and internally "feels" the shot with certainty. (How many times have you forgotten to look back at the hole one last time to stay connected to it, and then putted half the distance, just because your concentration was in the wrong hemisphere. You certainly were not picturing the distance of the hole.) Now he's ready to rely totally on his body to make the putt. And he strokes it, trusting that all his mental preparations will permit him to make a great stroke. Whether the putt drops is dependent upon other factors (such as bumpy greens) outside his control.

The key word here is *trust*. If our golfer were to demand internally that the putt drop, it could actually interfere with his execution. Even if the tournament championship were to ride on that one putt, the golfer could be better off making his preparations and trusting his body than demanding to himself that the putt drop. Self-demands are touchy. Some days you can "will" the ball into the hole, while on others, the same self-demand leads to pressing or choking. You will have to determine this. Considerations about what a putt means is totally irrelevant anyhow. Even the greatest "demander" of all time, Arnold Palmer, blew tournaments at his peak by overextending his skills. But he was willing to trade stunning wins for stunning losses.

4. "Instant compare." A split second after the shot is made, every top player physically "knows" whether he made the shot correctly or not. This is called *inner certainty*. You might say that you "feel" it when you made the right shot, and "know" it when you made the wrong shot.

5. "Post analysis." This occurs only if you are dissatisfied with the shot. You are likely to stay in this frame of mind and analyze what you did wrong, for too long a time. You may say aloud, "I pulled it," or "I rushed the line," or "I forgot about the condition." But it is best to quickly transform this verbal output into "feel" information, and a positive decision as to how to correct. Most physical errors are detectable and correctable immediately.

One of the most common mental errors is to continue this phase right into the next shot. This means you have continued to analyze the last shot instead of preparing yourself for the next. Golfers are notorious for "gagging" three-footers and then pumping their tee shots out of bounds. If, when preparing to make the next shot, you're thinking to yourself, "I've been pulling it, but this time I'm not going to," that's trouble. "Pulling" and "not" are negative words. Think affirmatively about what you intend to succeed in doing. Past and future reflections are counterproductive. Don't think backward.

Another point: If you make a really gross physical error, like dropping the ball early or missing the headpin by a wide margin, forget about it immediately. If you are a good bowler, then this kind of error is just a momentary lapse and doesn't warrant any analysis on your part.

PROFESSIONAL POINTERS ON THE MENTAL GAME

● Think optimistically—it's more profitable.
● A poor temper threshold comes from trying to overcontrol a percentage game.
● It's only after learning to control the ball that you discover the mental world of bowling.
● Expectation is the mother of frustration.
● Too much analysis will interfere with the greatest physical game.
● Muscles understand "feel," not words. So think "feel."
● Missing the shot in your mind guarantees missing it on the lane.
● Arguing with yourself ruptures inner certainty. Be fair with yourself. It helps maintain self-confidence.
● All of us have a genius for negative self-hypnosis. Don't think "error."
● Successful execution equals coupling the feel with picturing the shot.
● Think it, not *about* it.
● The ability to visualize comes from expanding your range—and vice versa.
● Be different—rationalize your successes, and analyze your failures.
● Keep the deliberation in your footwork and out of your mind.

SCIENTIFIC RESEARCH AND THE MENTAL GAME

Earlier I emphasized the point of not thinking too much, especially when the thoughts are negative. Research into biofeedback, which measures tiny electrical impulses created by the brain, has classified four types of brain waves. They are called delta, theta, alpha and beta waves. Delta waves are produced during deep sleep, theta waves during drowsiness and reverie, alpha waves during mental relaxation, and beta waves during mental effort and agitation. Alpha and beta waves are of interest to us.

When you are sitting down, "waiting in the wings," you should try to produce alpha waves, stay in an "alpha-wave state of mind." You can do this by consciously blanking your mind, or concentrating on one nonrelated thought. You might try slowing down your breathing, or thinking a single word or number over and over again. You can actually force your mind to relax by doing this. It will help you stay positively focused on what you're doing, without feeling panicky or agitated. However, if you are trying to figure out something, like finding a good lineup, then beta-wave activity will take place.

Also, there has been considerable research into which parts of the brain control which kinds of mental functioning. It has been discovered that in most cases the left half, or hemisphere, of the brain is the center for analytical, sequential, verbalized thinking. As you read this book, you are doing left-hemisphere work, unless you occasionally stop to "feel" a point that the book is making. If you read the book from cover to cover, over and over, and memorized all the material in it, you still wouldn't be able to bowl much better. You wouldn't have educated your *right* hemisphere, the center for "feel," muscle-memory, picturing, athletic and physical performance. Practicing a sport is mainly a right-hemisphere activity. Reading about it is left hemisphere.

Researchers think of people as "left-hemisphere (LH) oriented" or "right-hemisphere (RH) oriented." LH people tend to become the mental doers, the analyzers, the lawyers, the scientists, the computer programmers. They prefer to think of things in a symbolic way. They are good at thinking *about* things.

RH people are the physical doers, the athletes, the craftsmen, the commercial artists, the musicians (excluding composers). These right-hemisphere types are highly skilled with their hands and tend to think of how things are. It is natural for them to maintain concentration in the right hemisphere. Everyone uses both hemispheres. But some people prefer activities that belong to one hemisphere over the other.

In all cases, everyone uses both hemispheres every few seconds unless they intentionally *lock* their concentration into one hemisphere by excellent concentration. This is what the following discussion is all about: learning to detect and direct which hemisphere your concentration is in.

How do you *know* which hemisphere your concentration is in? Let's take a familiar example.

Try typing as fast as you can. Determine your maximum speed. When you were typing your fastest, you were not paying attention to the meaning of each word. Because maximum finger dexterity requires concentration solely in the right hemisphere, you don't have time to switch your attention back to the left side of your brain to decode the meaning of each word. Switching back and forth takes time and it will cause physical errors in typing. Understanding this physiological makeup of the brain is especially important when an athlete is trying to concentrate on executing a physical skill like throwing a strike in bowling (or baseball), or striking a golf ball correctly.

To prove this fact to yourself, try typing some other material as fast as you can. Only this time try to understand each word in each sentence and watch how your speed is reduced.

When you understand how something works, then control is possible. But if you don't, then you could be concentrating hard, but in the wrong hemisphere at the wrong time. You don't concentrate on words when trying quickly to do something physically complicated.

Other examples could be found in which reading about piano playing or bicycle riding is the only activity allowed. If that were the case, you wouldn't be able to ride a bike or play piano a lick. The right hemisphere still doesn't know how to balance the body while riding a bike until you permit it to practice.

LH people like to work through words or symbols. RH people like to work through their bodies (hands) and mentally picture events.

In sports, it is very important to have self-esteem. One way to develop self-confidence is by demonstrating a talent, but usually this is not enough. How many times have we observed a player fail who had all the tools but no confidence?

Just the same, you must also have a high regard for your mental abilities in addition to your physical talent.

The concept of I. Q. is misleading because it measures mainly left-hemisphere performance, which is fine for academic tasks. But what about the right hemisphere?

In the field of sports it is most important to have a high "right-hemisphere I. Q." A natural athlete has this. He learns sports automatically. He learns to deal with physical, spatial, and perceptual things rapidly. He doesn't have to read about the activity in order to learn it. Nor does he have to explain how he did it! He learns to coordinate his body skills quickly and successfully through personal experience.

The LH type of person is at a disadvantage initially because he learns physical execution more slowly, tends to fight himself psychologically—thinking the wrong thoughts at the wrong time—and lets analysis interfere with execution. If he continues this pattern of thinking he may never reach full potential. The LH type of athlete thrashes back and forth between both hemispheres, thinking it (RH) then *about* it (LH). He must work hard to maintain his RH concentration just prior to shot making.

Evidence that the LH (intellectual) takes longer to learn golf or bowling is seen in the amount of extra hours he practices. He'll be working on one idea, then on another. RH types find a good way and stay with it. They don't waste as much time trying several ways to accomplish the same task. In golf, LH types will vacillate, first trying to hit the ball straight, then trying to fade the ball, then drawing, then to fading again . . .

The worst problem an LH type of athlete has is when pressure is greatest. Then, he flips his concentration back over to his natural strength, the analytic left hemisphere, and begins an inner dialogue of commands. This is absolutely the worst way to execute good shots. The intellectually oriented: doctors, lawyers, and teachers are plagued with this curse. In golf, they are always complaining that they think too much over the ball.

LH and RH activity can interfere with each other if you don't discipline your mind. Of course, if you didn't know how your mind worked, it wasn't a case of discipline. At times, especially when you are reading a book like this or taking lessons, LH activity is predominant and necessary. But you must convert that analysis over to "feel." And the only way to do that is—you guessed it—PRACTICE. By practicing, you create feel. You reinforce the physical motion of making your approach and delivering the ball.

This is how the inner physical certainty is acquired. Your right hemisphere begins remembering, nonverbally, what the delivery feels like. If you encounter an extremely dry or oily lane condition, you must first analyze how to cope with the condition. *But then you must feel and picture how to do it.* It is necessary to stop thinking about the problem in words. Words are physical-execution killers.

What happens when you decide that there is something wrong with your physical game and you must change it? This is tough to do, because your left hemisphere must reeducate your right hemisphere. It is the left side that made the decision. If you've been bowling for a long time, your RH is going to resist this change. It won't like the new "feel"! Delivering the ball in a certain way has become a comfortable physical habit. It will take a lot of practice to break that habit and form a new, equally ingrained, and comfortable way of delivering the ball.

The lesson here is: Don't make drastic changes in your physical game unless you are *absolutely certain* that these changes have to be made. And then be prepared for a lot of practice, and a temporary disruption of a sense of "feel" in your delivery.

The barrier of comfortable "feel" blocks most people from successfully changing any part of their physical game in all sports. If you try to change your game, then don't expect to execute shots with a comfortable feel for the first fifty hours of practice. "Feel" comes gradually, not suddenly. If this doesn't occur, that's a signal that you are inducing the wrong physical change for your game. Therefore, either go back to your original game or, try a new idea.

10. THE MENTAL GAME— PART 2

Almost everyone would agree that you have to have some natural ability to become a good bowler. But there the agreement stops. When it comes to other essential qualities no two people will give you the same answer.

One person may say, "You've got to be able to concentrate completely on each shot." Another might disagree, saying, "No, that's not enough. It's practice that makes a good bowler. What good is natural ability if you don't develop it?" A third person will have still another opinion. However, there is no IT!

No one can tell you exactly what you'll have to work on to become a high-average bowler. But based on my own experience, I can offer a few suggestions in four areas: concentration and control; confidence and self-image; handling an opponent's needling; and practicing efficiently.

CONCENTRATION AND CONTROL

Prior to a Tournament / If you've bowled in the house before, forget about what happened in the past. If you've overheard other bowlers say the line is "outside," ignore it. If you've been told the lanes will be oiled in a certain way, don't believe it. Believe only what you see your ball do in the tournament itself.

During the Tournament / Concentrate on maintaining the touch that you developed in practice. Train yourself to concentrate on externals—hitting your target and figuring out the difference in each lane as you cross the house.

If you have committed yourself to trying your hardest, but find that you're throwing shots with less than your best effort, you probably need more work on developing mental stamina. Continue to think about external factors, like lining up and the cause of your problem. Don't worry or get angry.

Just before you get up to bowl, always make a firm decision about how to play the shot. It may be wrong, but indecision or arguing with yourself breaks concentration and results in a brief loss of confidence. At least, when a decision is made, you find out immediately if you were right or not. Good physical execution requires inner certainty. Don't act without it.

Channeling / Block out all thoughts that interfere with what you're trying to do. Concentrate on those things that make up your shot. If pressure causes extraneous thoughts to enter your mind, don't sit there and entertain them.

You control what you think about, if you want to. People do it in high-pressure situations all the time. Dictate to your imagination, not the reverse.

Concentration Without Control / Concentration alone is not enough. You must know what to concentrate on. You can concentrate in the wrong hemisphere, and on the wrong things: for example, thinking of how to fail.

Listen to successful people in any endeavor, sports or otherwise. Successful people do not like talking about how to fail. If you learn to keep successful thoughts in mind, you are likely to be successful.

Often in bowling you become so immersed in thinking about numbers that you forget to "feel." You become so engrossed in computing your back position and moving your target X-number of boards that you ignore just looking down the lane and picturing the shot that would benefit you the most.

The expert bowler who keeps his priorities straight adjusts faster. This means you always make pre-viewing the shot as it rolls down the lane a part of your mental picture. Don't translate what you see into a set of numbers and fail to get back to thinking and feeling the shot. Many a bowler has "spun out" just because he got too intellectual while bowling.

CONFIDENCE AND SELF-IMAGE

Confidence ebbs and flows like the tides. When you are sure of your game, mental strategies are irrelevant; and when you are not, that seems to be all you think about. Recap all your past pluses. If there aren't any, you're in the wrong sport.

Play Well Within Yourself / Try to work out a good shot; relax as if you're in a practice session when you've "got it going." Don't try to be perfect. Overcontrol wrecks your best shot. Don't set up expectations that automatically begin the internal mental war. You don't throw a strike every time you want in practice, so why expect more under the stress of pressure?

Be Decisive / Learn to live with your decisions. After you have thought out something, like a change in your floor position, stick with it throughout the execution of that shot. In searching for a good line, challenge your idea after you have thrown the ball and are able to assess the facts derived from the shot. Don't second-guess yourself while you are in the act of executing the trial shot or just prior to throwing the shot.

Performer vs. Spectator Thinking / Every person who competes in sports faces a common problem: When to think like a spectator, and when to think like a performer?

As the pressure increases in any situation, a natural reaction is to view yourself as others are viewing you. This is a luxury few can afford. Most bowlers will tighten up if they continually think of themselves the way fans do.

Bowlers have discovered and rediscovered that if they keep their minds channeled by concentrating on their game and leave spectating to the spectators, they will perform much better in the long run.

To be more specific, avoid such spectator thoughts as "If I get the next three strikes, I'll win . . ."; "If I strike out, I'll get my first 300 game," "I gotta get a double to win the game for my team—or what will they think of me?" And so on . . .

Another problem, peculiar to bowling and golf is that you can anticipate in advance what will be required to reach a specific goal. Whereas an outfielder doesn't know in advance that he is going to have to race back to the wall to spear a line drive, a bowler knows he must get twelve strikes to score 300. You must forget that and think one frame at a time, and one shot at a time. Leave thoughts about looking great to your friends in the crowd. It is perfectly natural to have your mind stray to thoughts that are counterproductive, but a professional trains his mind to behave unnaturally. ANY bowler can train his mind this way, but you should expect it to take a *couple of years* to complete the process of change.

THE MENTAL SNOWBALL

Don't allow yourself to get trapped in a mental snowball by not lining up properly. More than one problem originates from failing to solve this problem quickly.

Bowlers bowl by forming mental pictures of the line they are trying to play. For them, the importance of getting lined up quickly cannot be overstated, because if they fail to line up correctly they cannot make the mental picture appear. Without the confidence of the reality of this picture to guide your shots, it is easy to become confused.

When you are confused, your execution starts to break down. You either decide on wrong shots, or you can't think at all. In either case your execution becomes erratic and you lose your confidence.

With a temporary loss of confidence and erratic execution, reading lanes is impossible. Now you are faced with a monster. Instead of just one technical problem—that of finding the correct line—you have a complex set of problems. This is not an uncommon sequence of psychological events. So it behooves you to concentrate solely on getting lined up as quickly as possible.

This may sound extravagant but I've seen the situation carried to its extreme by some bowlers. After struggling with a bad line, they tend to think sarcastically: "Who needs it!" They think of ways to "bail out" or give up. This "giving up" is habit forming. Each time you do it, it makes giving up easier the next time. In this state of mind, all you're waiting for is a few bad breaks. Then it's bad-mouthing time: yourself, others, the game, etc.

I'm not going to say that it is just as easy to maintain your concentration as it is to give up, but learning to develop emotional stamina is just as important as developing physical stamina. Many players have developed the physical stamina to bowl sixteen to twenty games in one day, but still lack the emotional stamina to handle frustration for three games. So what good is all that practice and a fine swing, if your concentration and self-discipline give out?

DON'T BE DOGMATIC

For your confidence, it's important to realize that no one is perfect. There are some stubborn "I'm-always-right" high-190-average "experts" who never put it all together because of one problem: They lack ability to read lanes and interpret pin action. Their physical execution is fine, and they know a lot about the game. But this isn't enough. Learning to read lanes and learning how to follow oil requires sensitivity of the highest order. You cannot allow prejudices to block off information. Dogmatic bowlers continually force their prejudices onto the lanes when they should be keeping their minds open. You must allow the lanes to reveal where the line is by observing the lane's effect on the ball. You must adjust to the lane, instead of insisting the lane accept your line.

A bowler should be prepared to question his assumptions on how he plans to play a house. Some of the most experienced pros still get tricked. They misplay houses because they made up their minds in advance, forgetting that the house condition may have changed without their knowledge.

The ability needed to read lanes is similar to the skill of a frontier scout of the Old West in learning much from a few signs. In bowling, you can pick up small clues by noticing how your spare-ball reacted as it crossed the lane, by observing the pin action of another player, or by examining the residue of oil or finish on your ball.

Never close your mind to any source of information. Information alone cannot confuse a person who operates on sound theory.

PROFESSIONAL POINTERS ON COMPETITION

●Competition's emotional cripplers: temper, expectations, and unrealistic goals. The pins you throw away in anger now, when things are going wrong, will be regretted later, when things are going right.

●"I gotta get a double" signals trouble. One frame at a time, one shot at a time.

●When others are "lucking out," are you forgetting the breaks you got earlier in the game?

●A winner thinks only of how he can beat you. A loser worries about how to save face if he loses.

●Always expect to throw a strike, even if bad racks or spotty conditions interfere.

●Class is how you rank yourself. It shows.

●Lining up incorrectly negates all mental strategies.

●Train yourself to avoid distracting thoughts and outside emotional factors . . . or pay the consequences.

●If you have a set strategy for any given night, unset it. Keep an open mind.

●Analyzing why you are stroking so well is dangerous.

●Be modest if someone calls you a "superstar." Otherwise you'll think about your image instead of how to win.

●Cockiness is a poor substitute for confidence. Concentration prevents fear from controlling your mind, and thus eliminates the need for cockiness.

●Commit an "inexcusable" error, then see how long you brood about it. Winners always recover quickly.

●The last LH command should be: Picture the perfect shot.

NEEDLING

Some competitors build confidence in themselves by delivering successful needles to their opponents. This tactic seems to be particularly effective if the needle is funny, delivered in front of a group of people, goes unanswered, and if everyone laughs at the person being needled. Even when the target of the needle is largely unaffected, the needler himself may benefit by it. If the person who requires needling activity to bolster his confidence is not allowed to needle, his anxieties and imagination may get the best of him. He may not be able to get loose.

How do you distinguish playful banter from malicious needles? Did what was said leave you feeling good, or leave you feeling bad or puzzled?

Needlers use three methods:

1. Put-down statements: "Your game isn't good enough to be out here."

2. Attempts to gain information by probing questions: "How did you play the pair you just left?"

3. Mental stimulators designed to get an opponent to "think": "Did you know your armswing has a loop in it?"

Needlers usually lack the confidence to succeed with just their skills. They need an edge. They feel they can get this by putting the other player off balance. Sometimes it is done only to opponents to whom they feel inferior. At other times needlers needle anyone, just so they can relax at someone else's expense.

How Do You Handle a Needler? / The proper attitude is not to be guilty of throwing down the "first card." Don't issue the first statement of unpleasantries. A confident person doesn't need to be aggressive with his mouth.

However, once your "opponent" has made a move on you, there are three choices. Depending on your personality or style and the nature of the needle, (1) You can answer aggressively by being sarcastic, or neutralize his ploy by analyzing his behavior to him, sometimes with humor; (2) You can react passively by pretending to have missed his barb, and be unduly pleasant or even complimentary to him; or, (3) You can simply refuse to play his silly game and totally ignore him. But whatever choice you make, don't give validity to his statements with a defense of yourself.

THE QUESTION OF PRACTICE

At the physical level, bowling is a game of repetition. The ability to duplicate the same action with a minimum of error is the key to success. Naturally, a beginner finds it difficult to throw the ball the same way every time. A new bowler can see and understand the proper physical motion, but it may take a thousand repetitions before he can consistently execute the physical motion.

Every beginning bowler must develop the patience to put himself through endless drills. He must perform certain moves over and over again until they become natural actions. Coordination of footwork, armswing and release takes a long time to develop. But once you have overlearned a movement, you have it forever. This is true of any physical skill, whether it is dancing, riding a bike, or throwing a ball.

After you have learned a physically correct way to bowl, you can spend time on control and refinement. Scratch bowlers can get back in the groove relatively quickly after a layoff, while beginners flounder inefficiently during practice, searching for the correct way to execute—or developing methods they eventually abandon.

The concept of "muscle memory" is important here. Overlearning a skill like bowling involves developing muscle memory. If you try to recall a mental idea, you usually do it on the first attempt, even if you've only been exposed to the idea once. Physical memory, being more complicated, obviously takes much longer to develop, and within ten minutes it falls back to a state of "semi-recollection." This is why golfers waggle their clubs and take practice swings before hitting—to bring this semi-recollection back to a state of full recollection of feel. It also explains why bowlers "shadow bowl" before the competition begins. Unlike golfers, bowlers can't take "practice swings" immediately before throwing; they have one shot, and that's it. If the shot is wrong, they have to wait before throwing again.

Muscle memory begins to fade immediately after each shot. By practicing, you minimize the tendency for "feel" to fade away during competition. The more you practice—as long as you practice well—the more vivid your muscle memory becomes, and the more quickly it can be recalled at any given time. Thus, not only does practice improve your ability to execute; it gives you added confidence while competing. When the "feel" of the shot is ingrained, you don't have to think as much. *Practice, however, is not the complete answer.*

The best practicers do not always make the best bowlers. This is true for any sport. In order to excel, you must experience competitive situations that challenge you. In order to improve, you must bowl against bowlers who are as good as, or better than, you are. This is the only way to "steel" your nerves against the pressures of competition. A window washer doesn't overcome his fear of heights by washing only first-story windows.

If your average is now 175, and you're in a league where 175 is close to the top average, you're probably not going to improve. If you elect to stay at the same level and enjoy your reputation, you may become bored with the league and the game.

However, if you get into a league where 175 is only a medium average, you will grow. More will be expected of you. You will have a reason to strive for improvement, and you will certainly need that impetus to work on your game.

Always push against your "limits," and they won't be limits any more. The way to do that is to practice intensely and enter into higher levels of competition. Your scores are related to your execution, your ability to handle lane conditions—and the quality of the competition you face.

PROFESSIONAL POINTERS ON PRACTICE

●Practice makes perfect . . but only if you practice what is perfect for you.
●What you think while practicing determines what your thoughts will be under pressure.
●Practicing your strengths is fun, but where does that leave your weaknesses?
●Bad practice is worse than no practice. Those little muscle recorders never sleep.
●Concentrate intensely while practicing, and you'll be able to concentrate intensely while performing.
●For every good shot in competition, you must roll, literally, thousands in practice.
●Every time you attempt to implement a new idea in play, be prepared for the wheels to fall off over and over.

BOWLING'S DUALISM: "IT'S MY EXECUTION" VS. "IT'S THE CONDITION"

Whether consciously or not, most bowlers take one of these viewpoints. Each has its validity, but each has its blind spots too. Too rigid an attitude can distort your game, hold back your development, and restrict your performance in competition.

Which type are you? Could you improve your game by taking a balanced point of view? Here is a comparison of these two attitudes.

Execution-Oriented Bowler / This bowler believes that if he is to score, his execution must be nearly perfect. He emphasizes his physical game. He says: "When my execution is right, I can hit *any* condition." When things are going wrong, he tends to look for faults in his execution—timing, armswing, or release. He fails to line up well on a condition that doesn't favor his natural shot because he continues to focus on himself—his muscle feel, thought control, attitude, or how much rest he had the night before.

On the positive side, he quickly locates and corrects faults in his execution, provided he doesn't become overly concerned with perfection. His form is beautiful to watch. When the condition doesn't call for major adjustments, he scores easily.

But he retains a stubbornness to modify his game, and when the condition hurts his performance, he will blame it rather than trying to adjust to it.

Condition-Oriented Bowler / This bowler focuses his attention on lane conditions and pins. He isn't as concerned about his execution as long as it is correct at the point of delivery. He is more apt to find the line in a given house if it requires a major physical adjustment. But he is slow to recognize when something in his execution is wrong. He may have the confidence to try changing his physical game during competition, but he abandons his natural style too quickly—often to his detriment.

When advising another bowler who is having trouble, he will suggest experimenting with ball weights, grips and pitches, and will give pointers on lane reading. He will usually overlook execution problems both when advising and analyzing his own performance. When he falls into a slump, he will doggedly continue to emphasize factors outside himself, rather than focusing on the internal problem.

What's the answer to the problem? *Don't polarize!* Don't approach the game with one-sided mentality. There is both wisdom and foolishness in each point of view. In the old days, all the houses used shellac for a lane finish, and ABC rules stated that each house must resurface every other year or lose its sanction. Everybody played the second arrow (where a track developed to the pocket), all pins were made of wood (no plastics), and you had to develop a stronger release to blow the 5-pin. *At that time*, execution was the primary concern.

Now, however, we are in the modern era of bowling. Lanes may be coated with different types of finishes. They don't have to be resurfaced until the ABC inspector requests it. Pins are plastic or wood, and may have a high or low center of gravity. So now, in order to score well, players have to bowl anywhere from left of the fourth arrow to right of the first arrow.

In today's game, you should first work on your form. But you should also develop your ability to read lanes, interpret pin fall, and adjust to the myriad of lane conditions. It is a mental trap to think that either physical execution or adaptability to lane conditions alone is the complete answer.

The pros who are strong in both areas win the most money, year after year.

PROFESSIONAL POINTERS—AFTERTHOUGHTS

●Everyone wears two hats: performer and spectator . . . but you can only wear one in the clutch.

●Theorize as much as you want. Just don't forget to verify it in practice.

●Confidence is your best protection against the hazards of pressure.

●When you are stroking at your best, knowledge has your mind "channeled."

●Practice without concentration is worthless.

●Practicing strikes rather than practicing to line up creates a "condition-bowler."

●Did you ever practice bowling intentionally off the best line, so you could learn to recognize it more quickly?

●In league, bowl with people you like. It makes for a shorter season.

●When in trouble, search with confidence or make the most of your present angle.

●If you can't interpret pin action, you are always shadow bowling.

●How one manages his money is identical to how one manages his pin fall—throw pins away, throw money away.

● If you don't think equipment is important, let a 200 shooter lose his favorite ball.

● Tournaments are not won by "betting the favorite to show."

● "Frozen ropes" were invented by right-handed winners in brickyards.

● Development's obstacle: repetition and comfortable old "feels" followed by trial and error with its uncomfortable new "feel."

● If you have enough confidence to check out other scores, do it.

● Spares are made by being careful. Strikes are strung by being lined up.

● A runaway Brooklyn strike to win makes hypocrites of even the purest pocket shooters.

● If a slump persists after innovations fail, revert to a prior form that worked for you, or take a rest.

● Confidence is based on prior facts—your own track record. You can't con yourself with pep talks if the recent facts don't support it.

● Temper—the feeling that you are entitled to become upset. . . . Are you?

● Bad luck: Not being lined up.

● Efficiency: redirecting your emotions so that you win, not lose.

● A clear head adjusts faster.

● The spoiler usually has less pressure on him than the favorite, until *he* becomes the leader.

● You can sharpen your game through practice only so far. Then you have to get your head straight.

● Observations made while lined up are a hundred times more meaningful than those made while struggling.

● Don't wait for an opening. Force it.

● Everyone misses shots; only a few can accept this fact and still win.

● Be a poor loser . . . inside.

● The side of the brain you listen to music with is the side you want to control your bowling.

● The more attention you give to the point of release, the less you need in the pushaway.

● Calculation sets limits in the right half of your mind.

● Solving the line precedes setting your thoughts on automatic.

● Most players concentrate hard, but on the wrong things—such as fitting the shot.

● "Fight or flight" is the offspring of fear.

● An inner dialog while throwing the ball means the wrong side of your brain is in control.

● When your individual highest scores are better than your opponents' lowest scores you've got a chance for an upset.

●Tune in the pattern and tune out the rest.

●The ability to transfer—or not transfer—your concentration from one hemisphere to the other is what is meant by concentration.

●Focusing your mind is no different from focusing your eyes, except that the latter is automatic while the former requires training.

●Keeping track of your breath reduces pressure, while keeping track of your strikes builds pressure.

●Bowling with the wrong ball is like ice-skating with roller skates on.

●Some of the quietest people have the gabbiest minds.

●Hypnosis eventually wears off. Talent must then resume responsibility.

●Daydreaming is the enemy of concentration.

●Remember your inner conversations to see what you lack.

●"Blocked" lanes test nerves, brickyards test smarts.

●Two "if's," a "should have," and an "ought," define a loser.

●Before you decide to give up your style for a more classic style, think: Will this be quicker than figuring out the bugs in my own style?

●The most difficult thing in bowling is to reverse a total pin-fall tailspin in time.

●If eight in a row made a 300 game, many would squeeze the seventh.

●Brickyards make good bowlers look bad, bad bowlers look good . . . and left-handers look great.

●*If you don't enjoy it . . . give it up!!!*

CONCLUSION

We've covered a lot of ground together in the course of this book. We've gone from the basics of the sport to the lofty heights of professional technique and advanced theory. And along the way we've seen why it is that people say, "Bowling is an easy game to learn, but a difficult sport to master."

This is really the essence of bowling. For once you begin, you find there's so much to learn that no single person can ever hope to know it all.

Yet you and I and everyone else strive for perfection. We're constantly trying to improve our score.

That's what makes the sport so fascinating.It's why more than 65 million Americans go bowling every year and why bowling remains the most popular participant sport in the country. And, aside from the need to earn a living, it's one of the main reasons why professionals work so hard.

Everything covered here is designed to help you become a better bowler, to help you in your quest for perfection.

But *knowing* about bowling isn't enough. You've got to practice, practice, practice. You've got to work hard, and you've got to test yourself in competition.

And then, after all that work, after all the ups and downs and wins and losses, if you can *still* get excited about it, then without a doubt bowling is the right sport for you.